CLASSIC CHINESE COOKING

ANNA KAO

CLASSIC CHINESE COOKING

ILLUSTRATED BY
ROBERTA SCHWARTZ

A WALLABY BOOK
PUBLISHED BY POCKET BOOKS NEW YORK

Another *Original* publication of Wallaby Books

 A Wallaby Book published by
POCKET BOOKS, a division of Simon & Schuster, Inc.
1230 Avenue of the Americas, New York, N.Y. 10020

ISBN: 0-671-54080-7

First Wallaby Books printing January, 1985

10 9 8 7 6 5 4 3 2 1

WALLABY and colophon are registered trademarks
of Simon & Schuster, Inc.

Printed in the U.S.A.

To my husband Yu, for his love, patience, and strong stomach
during the twenty years I have developed my recipes.
I also feel most fortunate to have had the encouragement and honesty
of my dear children, Yuan, Joan, and Lisa.
To my friends, especially Veronica Volpe.
And to my many students, who helped me type, test,
and improve my recipes and my English.

CONTENTS

RECIPES

INDEX

�✻ |INTRODUCTION| ✻

THE CHINESE DIET

China's diet may be the diet of the future because it is high in nutrients, low in calories, and well balanced. It does wonders for weight problems: Its fish and seafood dishes are rich in protein; the meat dishes are low in fat; and its vegetable dishes, cooked quickly, retain maximum nutritional value. The Chinese diet does not include such dairy products as butter, cheese, cream and milk. Animal fats are rare, and vegetable oils are used for cooking.

A typical Chinese meal has about one-third the meat of an American meal. Instead of cooking roasts or steaks, the Chinese usually use bite-sized pieces or thin slices of meat, cooked with other ingredients. The Chinese eat more vegetables than Americans do, including soybean products, which are very high in protein.

Soy plays a large role in the Chinese diet. It is not only less expensive than other protein foods but it lends flavor to a long list of dishes. Chinese Buddhists and vegetarians can prepare banquets of a dozen or more dishes made with soy products. Among them are soybean milk, bean curd, bean sheets, bean cheese, soybean sprouts (different from the mung-bean sprouts known in the United States), soy sauce, soybean paste, and soybean oil.

The Chinese have a larger variety of vegetables available than many Americans realize. In addition to such familiar Chinese-restaurant offerings as bamboo shoots, water chestnuts, and snow peas, there is a large selection of leaf greens, beans, melons, and root vegetables.

The Chinese seldom eat sweet desserts and pastries, except at formal banquets. Instead, most families serve fresh fruit in season.

THE EASE OF CHINESE COOKING

The first thing I want to teach you about Chinese cooking is that it is *easy*—and in this book I will prove it. In addition to teaching you Chinese cooking techniques, I also want to teach you the importance of planning. You plan a menu; you must also plan the cooking steps. It is the planning that makes it easy. All you have to do is create your plan and follow it step by step.

All of my recipes are designed to let you fit them easily into the plans you create. They are divided into clear series of steps with specific notes on what is to be prepared ahead of time and what must be done when cooking. In my many years of teaching Chinese cooking, I have often turned a nervous novice into an eager enthusiast in just one lesson. My students tell me that what they like best about my recipes is the emphasis on planning: The way the recipes are presented forces them to organize themselves. You, too, must organize your cooking. When you know what ingredients are required, what must be done to them, and when you must take specific steps, you can create your plan. Planning will make you informed and organized instead of doubtful and confused. It is the key ingredient in successful cooking.

Decide what to cook, make a list of the ingredients needed, and find out where to buy them. If you have a list, it is easy to make changes should some ingredients be unavailable, or should your menu lack balance or variety.

When you have what you need, check the recipes for what must be done ahead of time. Meat, poultry, and seafood can be cut up, marinated, and stored in the refrigerator until needed. Some vegetables can also be cut up and stored in plastic bags ahead of time.

Mix your seasonings *before* you start cooking. That way you can taste them and make adjustments. You will have plenty of time if you have a plan.

Now you are ready to cook, with all of your ingredients prepared and near at hand. Always cook the meat and vegetables separately—the meat first, then the vegetables. When they are done, mix them together and add the seasonings. The dish is done! And it is guaranteed to be good, because you planned each step and followed your plan.

SPECIAL INGREDIENTS

Chinese cooking has become popular. A lot of ingredients that used to be sold only in Oriental food stores are now available in supermarkets, but some will still require a trip to an Oriental store.

Aside from fresh meats and vegetables, most ingredients used in Chinese cooking are imported. They are packaged in cans or jars, or are wrapped in plastic bags, and all should have long shelf lives. If you don't see what you want, ask the clerk (most of the time the owner, or a relative). If he doesn't have what you need, he may order it for you from the wholesaler.

Generally speaking, fresh foods are better than canned products, which are pre-cooked and processed, and may sometimes differ in taste or texture from fresh products.

Seasonings such as star anise and peppercorn are dried; they should last indefinitely. Hoisin sauce, fermented black beans and other seasonings are salted; they will last a long time under refrigeration. If they are packaged in cans, they should be transferred to glass or plastic containers after opening to prevent a reaction between the food and the metal.

The following is a list of special ingredients used in this book. Some will be unfamiliar to American cooks, and a few may be a bit difficult to find, depending on where you live. Do not fail to check gourmet shops and Hispanic and Italian markets, which sometimes stock some of these items. For your convenience, a list of stores is included in the next chapter.

INGREDIENTS

Agar-agar: A dried, flat, stringlike gum derived from seaweed and used as a vegetable in salads and in gelatinous dishes. Sold in packages by weight, it will keep indefinitely.

Baby corn: Tiny, tender, sweet ears of corn, 2–3 inches long. Used in stir-fried dishes and in salads. Available in cans, baby corn can be stored after opening: Cover with water and keep chilled, changing the water every other day, for about a week.

Bamboo shoots: About 3 inches across and 4 inches long, they are used in stir-fried dishes and soups. Available in cans, they can be stored after opening for about two weeks if kept chilled and covered with a fresh change of water every day.

Bean curd or bean cake: Square white cakes of solidified soybean milk, used in stir-fried dishes and soups. Available fresh or in cans, its consistency ranges from silky and jello-like to firm and springy. Keep chilled and covered with water, changed daily, for about a week. Pressed, dried or fried bean curd can be frozen 2–3 weeks, but the texture will change slightly.

Bean paste: A salty soybean product used as a seasoning. Available in cans and jars, it will keep six months or more under refrigeration.

Bean sprouts: Infant mung beans, cream-white when fresh and about 2 inches long (the fine roots at one end may be discarded). Used in stir-fried dishes, they are available fresh or pre-cooked in cans (canned bean sprouts should be rinsed before use). Fresh sprouts will keep 3–4 days under refrigeration. Canned sprouts will keep 2–3 days if drained, covered with fresh water and refrigerated.

Bean threads or cellophane noodles: Dried translucent noodles made from mung-bean starch. They must be soaked 5 minutes in water to soften. Bland, almost tasteless, bean threads are used in stir-fried dishes and soups because they absorb the flavors of other ingredients. Sold in packages by weight, they last indefinitely if kept dry.

Chili sauce or paste: A seasoning made of crushed dried chili peppers in salt and water or in a base of sesame-seed oil or soybean paste. Available in jars or cans, it will keep 2–3 months if refrigerated.

Chinese cabbage or celery cabbage: A delicate vegetable that resembles a fat bunch of celery. Used in stir-fried dishes and in soups, it is sold fresh and will keep 5–7 days refrigerated in a plastic bag.

Chinese mustard is the same as English mustard: a fine yellow powder that, when mixed with a little water, becomes fiery hot. Available dry in plastic bags or tin cans (pre-mixed Chinese mustard is sometimes found in jars, but is often unsatisfactory). Protected against moisture, it will last several months.

Chinese sausage: A cured and seasoned pork product that must be steamed 30 minutes before using. Sold in packages by weight; it can be frozen indefinitely in a plastic bag.

Dried chestnuts are used in pastries and in red-cooked chicken or pork dishes. Sold in packages by weight, they will keep indefinitely in the freezer.

Dried Chinese black mushrooms must be soaked in water to soften. Their delicate flavor adds to a wide variety of dishes. Sold in boxes and bags by weight, they will keep indefinitely in the freezer.

Dried chili peppers: Red hot, these require careful handling: Keep hands away from face and eyes, and wash hands thoroughly immediately afterward. In the pan, these peppers add a wonderful heat to many Szechuan and Hunam dishes. Sold loose or packaged, whole or crushed. They will keep indefinitely in a covered jar.

Dried seaweed is formed into thin sheets, often about 7 × 8 inches, and folded in half. Its salty, iodine-like taste is excellent in soups. Sold in packages by weight, it will keep indefinitely if protected against moisture.

Dried shrimp come already shelled and have a salty, fishy taste that adds to soups and vegetable dishes. Sold in packages by weight, they will last indefinitely in the freezer.

Chinese wood ears: Bland in taste, this black tree fungus must be softened in water before it is used in meats or vegetable dishes and in soups. Sold in packages by weight, they will last indefinitely in a jar or plastic bag.

Egg noodles are common in Chinese dishes, and any good dried egg noodles available in supermarkets will substitute adequately.

Egg-roll wrappers are available ready-rolled to the proper thinness and size—6 × 6 inches. Cut in quarters, they make perfect wonton wrappers. Available by the pound, chilled or frozen. They will keep only 2–3 days chilled but indefinitely when frozen.

Five-spice powder is a mixture of star anise, pepper, cinnamon, clove, and Szechuan pepper. Sold ready-mixed by weight, it keeps a long time in a tightly closed jar. If unavailable, substitute allspice.

Fresh hot peppers or banana peppers should be readily available in supermarkets.

Ginger: The root has a brown, scaly skin and pale, yellowish flesh; the taste is hot and slightly sour. The roots are sold by

14

weight; powdered ginger is also available on the spice shelf of any supermarket, but is at best an emergency substitute only. The root will keep a few weeks if chilled and wrapped; for better results, peel, slice, and soak in rice wine or dry sherry; cover tightly and refrigerate. It will keep six months or more.

Hoisin sauce is a seasoning blended of soybean paste, flour, sugar, garlic, and salt. It is excellent in stir-fried dishes, dips, and barbecue sauces. Available in cans and jars; covered, it will keep indefinitely under refrigeration.

Kumquats: Small, yellow-orange citrus fruit about 1½ inches long, with a tart orange flavor. Used as a dessert or garnish, and available in cans and jars. After opening, they will keep a few days under refrigeration, stored in their own syrup.

Lily buds or golden needles are light brown lily buds 2–3 inches long. Used in stir-fried dishes and in soups, they must first be softened in water. Sold in packages by weight, they will keep indefinitely if protected against moisture.

Longons or dragon's eyes: This cherry-sized fruit has a soft, brown skin, a sweet, creamy pulp, and a large pit, but is available in the U.S. (peeled and pitted) only in cans. It is used in desserts and will keep two weeks in a covered jar in the refrigerator.

Loquats are about the size of apricots; yellow and soft-skinned, they resemble peaches in taste and are used in desserts. Available pitted and peeled in cans. (Canned apricots or peaches may be substituted in a pinch.) Stored in their own syrup, they will keep almost two weeks under refrigeration.

Lotus roots: Brown in color and potato-like in shape, these water-lily roots are used in stir-fried dishes and in soups. They are available pre-cooked in cans, and also fresh or dried—but do not use fresh or dried for recipes in this book, as the flavors and textures are different. Will keep 2–3 weeks in the refrigerator.

Lotus seeds are ivory-colored and shaped like peanuts. Used in soups, as decorations in sweet dishes, and as pastry filling, they are available dried in boxes. They will keep indefinitely in the freezer.

Lychees may sometimes be called lychee nuts, but they are not nuts at all. They are a fruit with a soft red shell and they look a little like strawberries. Inside, they have a sweet, tender pulp that enhances sweet-and-sour dishes and desserts, and can also serve as a garnish. Available peeled and pitted in cans, they will last about 2 weeks in their own syrup under refrigeration.

Oyster sauce: A thick, brown sauce made from oysters, and used as a seasoning in stir-fried dishes and in dipping sauces. It is available in jars and cans, and will keep indefinitely under refrigeration.

Red-bean paste: A sweetened puree of red soybeans used as a filling in pastries and desserts. Sold in cans, it will keep 6 months or more if transferred to a jar and refrigerated.

Rice flour is used in pastry batter and sweet dishes, and is sold in boxes by weight. It will keep for months in a tightly covered jar and indefinitely in the freezer.

Rice sticks: These thin and brittle noodles must be soaked in water before they are used. Common in stir-fried dishes and in soups, they are also deep-fried for use as a garnish. Sold in packages by weight, they keep indefinitely in a plastic bag.

Salted black beans: Strongly scented fermented black beans, which may be rinsed before use as a seasoning in meat, poultry, and seafood dishes. Available in jars, cans, and plastic bags, they will keep indefinitely if tightly covered.

Sesame seeds: Small, fat, white seeds used as a seasoning and as a garnish. Sold loose or in bottles or bags. Will keep indefinitely if tightly covered.

Sesame-seed oil: A brown oil with a nutty flavor, used as a seasoning in sauces or as a salad dressing. Will keep indefi-

15

nitely in the pantry, tightly covered in a dark place.

Sesame-seed paste: A paste with the consistency of peanut butter (which may be substituted in a pinch). Used as a seasoning and in cold dishes and salad dressings. Sold in jars, it will keep for months tightly covered and refrigerated. Can be made at home (page 41).

Star anise: A licorice-flavored spice in the shape of an eight-pointed star. Used as a seasoning ingredient. Sold loose or in packages, by weight; will last indefinitely if tightly covered.

Straw mushrooms: Small in size; yellow and black in color; silky in texture; and bland in taste. Straw mushrooms are used for decorative effect to enrich the color of stir-fried dishes. Sold in cans, they must be refrigerated in a jar of water after opening.

Sweet rice or glutinous rice: A short, round-grained rice; the grains tend to stick together when cooked. Used as a poultry stuffing and in desserts. Sold by weight. Will keep for months in the pantry and indefinitely in the refrigerator.

Sha cha sauce: A dark brown paste of ground peanuts, garlic, dried shrimp, sugar, salt, and spices. Used as a seasoning in barbecued and stir-fried dishes. Sold in cans and bottles, it will keep a few months tightly covered and refrigerated.

Shark's fin: Translucent threads of dried shark cartilage. Must be softened in water and rinsed before use in soups and meat or poultry dishes served at banquets and formal dinners. Sold in boxes by weight or canned and partially prepared in chicken stock. Will last indefinitely in the pantry, protected against moisture.

Shrimp chips: These dried chips of shrimp-flavored dough must be deep-fried before serving (page 42). Used as an appetizer and a garnish, they are sold in packages by weight and will keep indefinitely.

Snow peas: Flat green pea pods picked before the peas develop inside. Tender but crisp, with a sweet taste, they need little cooking and are featured in stir-fried dishes. Sold fresh by weight, they will keep two weeks refrigerated in a plastic bag.

Soy sauce: A salty brown liquid from fermented soybeans. Light soy sauce is the most delicate and flavorful; dark soy sauce is thick with molasses; and medium soy sauce falls in between. The light is used at the table or to season dishes without changing their color. Medium and dark are used in cooking only. Sold in bottles and cans ranging from a few ounces to a gallon, it will keep indefinitely in the pantry.

Sweet rice powder or glutinous rice flour is milled from sweet (glutinous) rice and used in batters, pastries, and desserts. Sold in boxes and packages by weight. Store in a covered jar; it will keep for months in the pantry and indefinitely in the freezer.

Szechuan peppercorns: Tiny, reddish-brown, and pleasantly scented, they are much stronger than ordinary black peppercorns. Sold in packages by weight, whole or ground. Whole peppercorns will keep indefinitely if tightly covered.

Szechuan pickles: A salted, preserved, vegetable root; its color varies from yellow to green. Used as a condiment or seasoning, it is available in jars and cans by weight. Covered and refrigerated, it will keep indefinitely.

Tangerine peel: The dried rind of mandarin oranges. It must be softened in water before using as a seasoning ingredient in soups and meat or poultry dishes. Sold in packages by weight, it will keep indefinitely in the pantry if protected against moisture.

Water chestnuts: About the size of roasting chestnuts, they are actually bulbs. The skin is thin and brown; the cream-colored meat is crispy and sweet. They may be eaten raw or cooked, and are often used in stir-fried dishes. Available in cans, they will keep a few weeks under refrigeration in a covered jar with water (change water twice a week).

Water-chestnut flour is used in batters and as a thickener for sauces. Sold in packages by weight, it will last indefinitely in a covered jar.

Winter melons are about the size of small watermelons, with frosty green skin and bland, white meat within. Used in stir-fried dishes and in soups. Sold fresh by weight, whole or in sections. Sections will keep up to 5 days, wrapped and refrigerated. Whole melons will keep for months in a cool, dark place.

Wonton wrappers: The same as egg-roll wrappers (from which they may be cut), but 3 × 3 inches in size.

SOURCES OF SUPPLY

The following list may assist you in shopping for ingredients. Stores marked with an asterisk will accept mail orders.

ARIZONA
Phoenix Produce Company
202 South Third Street
Phoenix, Ariz. 85004

*Roland's
1505 East Van Buren
Phoenix, Ariz. 85026

CALIFORNIA
*Chong Kee Jan Company
838 Grant Avenue
San Francisco, Calif. 94108

*Kwong on Lung Importers
680 North Spring Street
Los Angeles, Calif. 90012

*Wo Soon Product Company
1210 Stockton Street
San Francisco, Calif. 94133

Wing Chong Lung Company
922 South San Pedro Street
Los Angeles, Calif. 90015

FLORIDA
South Eastern Food Supply
6732 N.E. Fourth Avenue
Miami, Fla. 33138

GEORGIA
Asia Trading Company
2581 Piedmont
Atlanta, Ga. 30324

HAWAII
Tai Yen Company
1023 Maunkea Street
Honolulu, Hawaii 96817

ILLINOIS
Kam Shing Company
2246 South Wentworth Street
Chicago, Ill. 60616

Oriental Food Market
7411 North Clark Street
Chicago, Ill. 60657

Star Market
3349 North Clark Street
Chicago, Ill. 60657

INDIANA
A.B. Oriental Grocery
3709 Suit Shadeland Avenue
Indianapolis, Ind. 46226

MARYLAND
Asia House Grocery
2433 Saint Paul Street
Baltimore, Md. 21218

MASSACHUSETTS
Wing Wing Imported Groceries
79 Harrison Avenue
Boston, Mass. 02111

Chong Lung
18 Hudson
Boston, Mass. 02111

MICHIGAN
*Chinese Asia Trading Company
734 S. Washington Road
Royal Oak, Mich. 48067

*Seoul Oriental Market
23031 Beach Road
Southfield, Mich. 48075

Lun Yick
1339 Third Avenue
Detroit, Mich. 48226

MISSOURI
King's Trading
3736 Broadway
Kansas City, Mo. 64111

Lung Sing Company
10 South Eighth Street
St. Louis, Mo. 63102

NEW YORK
Kam Man Food Products Company
200 Canal Street
New York, N.Y. 10013

*Southeast Asia Food Trading Company
68 A Mott Street
New York, N.Y. 10013
(mail-order minimum $15)

*Little Mandarin Food Inc.
80 Fifth Avenue
New York, N.Y. 10011
(mail order minimum $7.50)

*Wing Fat Company
33–35 Mott Street
New York, N.Y. 10013

OHIO
Crestview Foodtown
200 East Crestview Road
Columbus, Ohio 43202

*Soya Food Products
2356 Wyoming Avenue
Cincinnati, Ohio 45214

Friendship Enterprises
3415 Payne Avenue
Cleveland, Ohio 44114

PENNSYLVANIA
Asian Merchandises, Inc.
707 Penn Avenue
Wilkinsburg, Pa. 15221

Hon Kee Company
935 Race Street
Philadelphia, Pa. 19107

Sambok Oriental Food
1737 Penn Avenue
Pittsburgh, Pa. 15222

TEXAS
*Oriental Import-Export Company
2009 Polk Street
Houston, Texas 77003

WASHINGTON
Wak Yong Company
416 Eighth Avenue, South
Seattle, Wash. 98104

WASHINGTON, D.C.
Da Hua Foods
615 I Street N.W.
Washington, D.C. 20001

*Mee Wah Lung Company
608 H Street N.W.
Washington, D.C. 20001

CANADA

ONTARIO
Wing Tong Trading Company
137 Dundas Street W.
Toronto, Ontario
Canada M5G 1Z3

QUÉBEC
Leong Jung Company
999 Clark Street
Montreal, Québec
Canada

UTENSILS

I feel strongly that it is not necessary to buy Chinese utensils. Ordinary utensils often serve just as well. You probably already have everything needed for almost every recipe in this book: a large skillet, assorted saucepans, a sharp knife, and a cutting board. If a steamer is called for, you can easily improvise one following the instructions later in this section.

But if you are going to cook Chinese dishes frequently, you may wish to buy at least the three basics: the wok, the cleaver, and a few pairs of chopsticks. All are inexpensive, and are available in Oriental stores and many department stores. They will make you more efficient and provide an incentive to "cook Chinese" more often.

THE WOK

The wok is a round-bottomed metal bowl made in sizes ranging from 12 to 25 inches in diameter (14 inches is standard for household use). They are available in copper, stainless steel, and aluminum, but the plain, carbon-steel wok is the one most often found in Chinese restaurants and homes: It is cheap, durable, and easy to clean.

Woks are sometimes sold in boxed sets that include a domed lid and a wok ring. The lid is useful in steaming and braising (for steaming, a bamboo steamer is put inside the wok, but a round cake rack will suffice). The ring stabilizes the wok when it is used on an ordinary kitchen gas or electric range. On some ranges, the ring may raise the wok too high above the burner for stir-frying—but you should experiment before deciding not to use it. It is important, for safety's sake, that any cooking vessel be stable on the stove, especially when you are cooking with hot oil. (Flat-bottomed woks are becoming available, though they are not yet common. The flat bottom, which should be three or four inches across, eliminates the need to use a wok ring on the stove.)

The wok is perfect for stir-frying: It provides a large cooking surface, but requires very little oil. It is also good for pan-frying, parboiling, simmering, braising, and deep-frying. It is a good—and inexpensive—investment. If you buy only one piece of Chinese cooking equipment, it should be a wok.

New woks should be scrubbed clean (many come with a light coating of inedible protective oil) and then seasoned: Brush oil all over the inside and heat the wok over low heat until it is hot. Allow the wok to cool to room temperature, then wipe out any excess oil with an absorbent cloth.

You may use peanut oil or other salad oil for wok cooking. Peanut oil is best, because it gives more flavor.

After use, clean your wok with hot water and a scrub brush. (Do not use soap—you will have to season the wok all over again.) As a cleaning aid you can use table salt, as you would for a good cast-iron skillet. Carbon-steel woks should be towel-dried to prevent rust.

THE CLEAVER

The Chinese cleaver is a multi-purpose cutting tool. It has a 4″ × 8″ rectangular blade and a 3- or 4-inch handle of wood or steel.

There are two kinds of cleavers. The first, thin and razor-sharp, is used for slicing and shredding. Any sharp and fine-quality chef's knife can be used instead.

The second kind is a heavy tool used for chopping bones, cutting whole poultry or lobster, or chopping or mincing meat. Any Western-style cleaver will suffice.

Both kinds of cleaver are made of either carbon steel or stainless steel. Carbon-steel cleavers may rust unless dried thoroughly after each use and rubbed with vegetable oil from time to time. (Before using a new carbon-steel cleaver, scrub it carefully to remove all traces of its protective oil coating.)

With either kind, the flat of the blade is used to scoop chopped food from the cutting board. It is also used for pounding and tenderizing meat, and crushing garlic, ginger, and radishes. A slight blow with the flat of the cleaver makes it easy to peel a clove of garlic.

CHOPSTICKS

Chopsticks, which add greatly to the pleasure of eating Chinese food, are easy to master with a little practice. Most are made of bamboo, but plastic chopsticks are becoming common in Chinese restaurants because they can be easily sterilized for re-use. The plastic variety, however, are rather slippery, which is annoying not only to novices but even to some Chinese. Both kinds are readily available in Oriental stores, and are very cheap.

Table chopsticks are about 10 inches long. They are squared at the "handle" end and rounded at the tip. Longer cook's chopsticks are also available, and can be very handy for manipulating small bits of food during cooking.

THE STEAMER

There are metal steamers and bamboo steamers. A metal steamer comes with a large saucepan for a base; a bamboo steamer has no base, and sits in a wok.

A basic steamer has three parts: a vessel that holds boiling water, a rack for the food, and a tight-fitting lid to prevent the steam from escaping too easily. The water should be at least two inches below the rack, so it will not splash onto the food. When steaming food for long periods, check the water level occasionally: You may have to add more boiling water to avoid burning the pot. Rising steam cooks the food evenly, so there must be adequate room between the food and the lid for the steam to circulate freely.

THE HOME-MADE STEAMER

You can easily improvise if you don't have a steamer.

A round cake rack will work effectively in a wok. You can also put a handleless metal strainer or colander in a large pot.

The simplest thing is to buy an inexpensive folding-leaf steaming rack, which should be available at any store that carries kitchen utensils. These racks are well perforated and are footed to hold the food above the water. They are about five inches wide, and their folding leaves open like a flower blossom to fit pots up to about nine inches in diameter.

Aluminum Steamer

Bamboo Steamer

THE LONG-HANDLED SCOOP AND THE SPATULA

These are perfect for stir-frying. Because of the round bottom of the wok, the long-handled scoop and spatula, which have slightly rounded edges, are most efficient in cooking foods with sauces. Large kitchen spoons and spatulas can be used instead, but if you decide to buy a wok, buy wok utensils too.

THE STRAINER

Some stir-fried dishes require draining during cooking. The strainer is suitable for this purpose, and can also be used to drain noodles, deep-fried food, and whole poultry and fish. Chinese strainers are round, with shallow bottoms of perforated metal or wire mesh. Generally larger than American strainers, they vary in size from five to fifteen inches, have handles, and are made of carbon steel, aluminum, stainless steel, or brass wire. The strainer is placed over a large bowl, which catches the drippings.

Any large Western-style sieve or colander can be used instead.

CUTTING

Chinese cooking is quick cooking because all ingredients are cut into bite-sized pieces. You may find this tedious and time-consuming at first, and if you have ever watched the knifework of a skilled chef, you may find it intimidating. But your skill and enthusiasm will improve. All you need is practice—and sharp knives.

To start, have all of your ingredients ready. Meat and chicken are easier to cut if well chilled, which makes them firm and less likely to move under your blade. Some cooks go so far as to have their meat semifrozen, which can be helpful when a recipe calls for very thin slices, but it calls for extra planning. You must plan the freezing, and then leave time for the meat to thaw fully after you cut it up.

To prepare seafoods, wipe them down with a little sherry mixed with salt—to remove the fishy odor—and then rinse in water.

Make certain your cutting board is rock-steady. If it slips in use, it will be dangerous. A well-moistened kitchen towel between board and countertop will solve the problem.

Your knife or cleaver must be sharp. The important thing to remember in cutting is that you *hold* the knife in one hand but *guide* it with both. Hold the knife gently but firmly. The thumb and index finger lightly grip the top edge of the blade just ahead of the handle. The other fingers grip the handle, lightly holding it in the groove between your thumb and palm. This grip, which all professional chefs use, gives you great control.

The other hand holds the food, and also guides the knife. Curl your fingers back slightly, so only their tips touch the food, and rest the flat of your blade against your knuckles. Both hands move in concert—the knife hand doing the cutting, the other moving back steadily, determining the width of the piece to be cut. If you never raise the blade above the level of your knuckles, you will never cut yourself, because your fingertips are curled away from the blade, which is kept at a safe distance by your knuckles.

Proceed slowly at first, and always watch your hands as you cut. Soon you will gain confidence and begin to pick up speed. Eventually you will have a skill you are proud of.

Pieces should be cut to approximately the same size—something you will get better at with practice—so they will cook evenly.

In dishes containing both meat and vegetables, the meat determines the cutting: If it is shredded, all other ingredients are shredded, for example.

Why so much cutting? There is not one reason but several. Small pieces mean speedy cooking, because more surface area is exposed to the heat. That saves fuel and time. Tough meat is tenderized when cut into small pieces. Ingredients retain more of their natural taste, color, texture, and food value when cooked only briefly. In the end, a little extra cutting makes cooking much simpler.

SLICING

Use a Chinese cleaver or a Western-style chef's knife with an 8-inch blade (a 6-inch blade is often too small for speed and convenience; a 10-inch blade is too large, except for experts). Do not use a slicing knife—its blade is too narrow to permit you to use your knuckles as a guide, as described earlier in this section.

The average slice called for in this book is about 2 inches long, 1 inch wide and $\frac{1}{8}$ to $\frac{1}{5}$ of an inch thick. Meat should be sliced across the grain for tenderness.

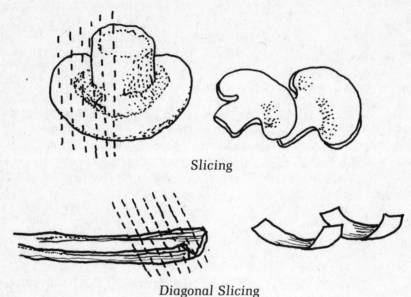

Slicing

Diagonal Slicing

JULIENNE (Match Sticks)

First cut slices of meat or vegetable $\frac{1}{4}$ of an inch thick, then cut the slices into match sticks, also $\frac{1}{4}$ of an inch wide, about 2 inches long.

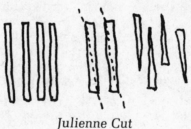

Julienne Cut

SHREDS

These pieces are even finer than match sticks. After cutting slices $\frac{1}{4}$ of an inch thick, lay the slices flat on the board and cut into strips about $\frac{1}{8}$ of an inch wide.

As you become more skillful with the knife, you will be able to shred several slices at a time. The preferred method is to make an offset stack, with each slice resting partly on the slice below it and partly on the cutting board. That keeps the slices from sliding as you cut them.

DICE, CUBES, AND CHUNKS

No matter which you make, three cuts are required, all of the same size. For example, dicing means cuts of about $\frac{1}{3}$ of an inch, in this sequence: First cut $\frac{1}{3}$-inch slices; cut the slices into $\frac{1}{3}$-inch strips; cut the strips into $\frac{1}{3}$-inch squares. The result: dice measuring $\frac{1}{3}$ of an inch on all sides.

Cubes measure $\frac{1}{2}$ inch to 1 inch on all sides.

Chunks measure $1\frac{1}{2}$ to 2 inches.

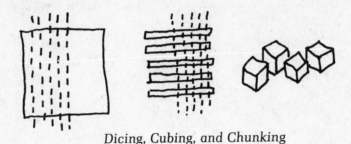

Dicing, Cubing, and Chunking

CHOPPING

Chopping reduces food to pieces about $\frac{1}{4}$ of an inch square. Vegetables can be chopped with the knife or with a hand-operated vegetable chopper; for chopped meat, a meat grinder with a coarse setting is good.

For both chopping and mincing (below), be cautious about using food mills or food processors. Either may turn food into a mush or purée, which will cook far too quickly and may burn.

MINCING

This is very fine chopping. The knife can be used, as can a hand-operated vegetable chopper or a meat grinder. Be careful about using a food mill or a food processor (see Chopping, above).

ROLL CUTTING

Roll cutting produces wedge-shaped pieces that expose extra surface area in cooking; breaks up the fibers in stringy vegetables for added tenderness; and provides a decorative effect. It is appropriate with long, narrow vegetables, such as carrots.

Make all cuts at an angle of about 30 degrees; after each cut, give the vegetable a one-quarter turn and cut again; the result is a bite-sized wedge.

Roll Cutting

SCORING

Large pieces of meat or whole fish are scored with a knife or cleaver; the shallow incisions speed the penetration of the seasonings and reduce cooking time. Scoring may be done in diamond or square patterns for decorative effect as well.

The depth of the incisions varies; generally it is halfway to the bone for fish and a half-inch to an inch for meat. The incisions should be about an inch apart, and may be vertical or, to expose more surface area, at a 45-degree angle.

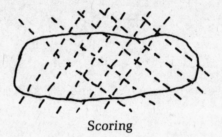

Scoring

MARINATING AND SEASONING

In marinating, meat, poultry, or seafood is steeped in mixtures that include egg, corn starch, wine, salt, soy sauce, sugar, pepper, and oil.

Marinades have many uses. They seal in juices and flavor: Meat marinated in egg and corn starch tends to be tastier and have a smoother texture. They also tenderize meat (tenderized meat can tolerate a little overcooking without becoming too tough), add their own flavors, and enrich the colors of other ingredients. They can counteract the fishy odor of seafood, and they make stir-frying easier: Marinades with oil keep pieces of meat separate.

Unmarinated meat dishes may be rather bland; they have only meat and sauce to provide flavor. Such dishes often depend on gravies heavily thickened with corn starch.

Marinating must be done ahead of time, so planning is required, but you have some flexibility here. Marinades have a preserving effect that allows meat to be kept under refrigeration for several days.

Marinades work faster at room temperature, but warmth increases the chance of bacterial activity. Room-temperature marinades should therefore be used only in dishes that are to be cooked.

Chinese dishes are seasoned before serving, not at the table, leaving you little time to taste and correct the seasoning. This is particularly true of stir-fried dishes, which cook quickly and must be served piping hot. For that reason, mix and taste your seasonings before cooking begins.

COOKING METHODS

STIR-FRYING

The most common method in Chinese cooking, stir-frying is fast and simple. Bite-sized ingredients are cooked in a hot wok or skillet with just a little oil while the cook stirs constantly. Speedy cooking preserves the color, taste, and texture of the ingredients. Stir-fried dishes look good, taste good, and smell good.

But speed requires organization and planning. You must have all ingredients laid out near to hand—there won't be time to hunt for something you forgot about.

In all meat-and-vegetable dishes, cook the meat first, then remove and set aside. Only two or three tablespoons of oil will be necessary for meat. Add the vegetables by cooking time: long-cooking vegetables first, quick-cooking ones (leafy spinach, for example, and fragile, high-moisture zucchini) last. Vegetables require even less oil: Two tablespoons are enough for a pound.

Don't crowd your wok. Give the food plenty of room to move in—and keep it moving constantly.

After the vegetables have been stirred through the oil and well coated, add the seasoning sauce; when they are almost completely cooked, return the meat to the wok and blend the ingredients briefly to mix the flavors and bring the meat up to the proper temperature.

Serve immediately. The dish will suffer if allowed to linger, even off the heat. The food will continue to cook in its own heat, so it is better to undercook a little bit than to overcook in the slightest.

NOTE: If stir-fried dishes call for draining, remove food from wok or skillet with a strainer or slotted spoon. Refrigerate extra oil for future use.

STEAMING

Steaming, another popular cooking method in China, cooks food without the use of oil. Steamed dishes retain all of their natural juices and flavors. Steam is used to cook rice, meat, poultry, seafood, buns, dumplings, pastries, and custards.

The constant temperature of steam heat keeps food moist and tender, but it also means cooking times can run from 15 minutes to several hours, depending on the ingredients. During long periods of steaming, check the water level from time to time to prevent burning the pot. If water is needed, add *boiling* water only. To increase cooking capacity and to save time by cooking several different dishes at once, a multi-layered Chinese bamboo steamer can be used.

To prevent overcooking, the food should be removed from the heat as soon as it is done. First, turn off the heat. Then remove the lid, and wait for a few seconds to let the steam escape before removing the platter. Always use gloves or mitts. Steamed food may go directly from the steamer to the table.

RED-COOKING

Red-cooking uses soy sauce to produce a reddish-brown gravy. The ingredients are browned in oil, then seasoned with sherry, ginger, scallions, star anise, etc., and simmered in a small amount of liquid in a covered pot over low heat.

This method is usually used with large cuts of pork or beef, whole poultry, bean curd, and fish. If vegetables are called for, they should be added at the last minute to preserve crispness.

Red-cooked dishes can be prepared in advance and refrigerated. Their flavor may improve with reheating. The sauce can serve as gravy for noodles and rice. The meat can also be served chilled (the sauce then becomes jellied) as cold cuts or appetizers.

SIMMERING

Simmering is the slow cooking of food in liquid at a temperature a few degrees below the boiling point for a long period of time. Stews and soups are simmered, not boiled.

One advantage of simmering is that it is gentle, and will not destroy the shape of your ingredients. Another is that it will cook high-protein foods such as meat, poultry, and seafood without toughening them. In fact, a long simmering will turn tough meat tender.

DEEP-FRYING

Deep-frying is done in two ways.

Partial cooking: Drop shredded, sliced, or cubed food that has been marinated into warm or hot oil (peanut or other salad oil) to fry for thirty to sixty seconds; stir constantly and drain immediately. The partially cooked pieces won't stick together when fried to doneness later.

Full cooking: Drop food coated with corn starch, flour, or batter into oil. The cooking time and temperature depend on the ingredients. They are done when golden brown, and should be drained immediately.

The temperature of oil for deep frying is usually from 325 to 375 degrees Fahrenheit. Test with an oil thermometer or by dropping a small piece of bread crust into the oil: If it sizzles, the oil is hot enough.

Properly deep-fried food forms a tasty, crispy coating that seals in flavor and absorbs a minimum of oil. Success requires keeping your oil at the proper temperature. If you use too little oil, or add ingredients in large amounts, the temperature will fall too quickly, and soggy food will be the result. Add ingredients slowly, in small amounts. Let them swim freely in plenty of oil.

Oil from deep frying may be strained and saved for re-use. Oil used for seafood should be kept apart from others and re-used only for seafood.

NOTE: When deep-fried foods call for draining, remove food from wok or deep-fryer with chopsticks, tongs, or a slotted spoon, holding food over wok to let most of the oil drip off. Then dry on paper towels.

ROASTING

Roasting is one of the oldest of all cooking methods. Roasting in China was formerly done in large outdoor ovens, with the meat or poultry turned on a spit or hung high over the fire. Indoor roasting is now usually done in an oven or over coal. It can also be done outdoors with an electric rotisserie over charcoal.

Roasting serves to cook large cuts of pork and whole poultry. Poultry skin is dried and pork is usually marinated for roasting. Both should be seared briefly in a very hot oven to form a crust, then roasted slowly until done at the right temperature—generally 300–350 degrees Fahrenheit. For self-basting, poultry is placed breast side up, pork, fat side up, on a rack in a shallow pan. Put an inch of water in the roasting pan to catch the grease and to prevent spattering.

Chinese roasted meats and poultry are always juicy inside and crispy outside.

REGIONAL COOKING STYLES

There are six major Chinese cooking styles: Peking (or Mandarin), Cantonese, Szechuan, Hunan, Fukien, and Shanghai. Their differences, and examples of their special dishes, are listed separately below:

PEKING (OR MANDARIN) STYLE

Peking, in the north, has been and still is the capital of China. It is also the country's greatest cultural and intellectual center. For centuries, many fine chefs migrated to Peking to seek an opportunity to serve the King and his high-ranking officials. Therefore, the Peking style is linked to formal dinners and banquets. It has both mildly seasoned and strongly flavored dishes. It uses dark soy sauce and a great deal of garlic, onion, leek, Chinese chives, and bean paste. Specialties include Peking Duck, Chicken Velvet, Moo Shu Pork, and Spring Roll (or Egg Roll).

The North, including the surrounding regions of Shantung, Mongolia, and Manchuria, has the country's best dumplings, noodles, and steamed breads. The Peking and Shantung styles are almost indistinguishable from each other. The people of Mongolia and Manchuria are nomadic; their cooking is characterized by such dishes as Mongolian fire pot and barbecued lamb.

CANTONESE STYLE

Canton is a port on China's southern coast; its cooking is well-known in many nations. The Cantonese introduced Chinese cooking to the West, establishing restaurants almost everywhere. Cantonese cuisine is colorful and characterized by its fidelity to the natural taste of each ingredient and its subtle blends of flavors. It emphasizes quick cooking, with very little seasoning. The Cantonese developed the techniques of stir-frying, steaming, and roasting. They originated the concept of the teahouse, where people gather to drink tea and eat dim sum (richly varied appetizers) while talking business, politics, and weather from dawn to dusk. Specialties include: Cantonese Roast Duck, Beef in Oyster Sauce, Steamed Fish, Lobster Cantonese, and Sweet and Sour Pork.

SZECHUAN STYLE

Szechuan is in southwestern China. The provincial capital is Chungking, which was also the national capital during World War II. In this hilly region of fierce winters, the people like hot, peppery dishes. They use ginger, garlic, Szechuan peppercorn, and red-hot peppers in dishes that are hot, highly spiced, and oily. Specialties include: Palace Chicken, Double-Cooked Pork, Yu Hsiang Pork, and Paper-Wrapped Chicken.

HUNAN STYLE

Hunan, in central China, also offers dishes that are spicy and rich with seasonings. The Yang-Tze River runs through the province; its carp and other freshwater seafood inspired Hunan Crispy Fish, a fried dish sauced with vinegar and sugar. Other specialties include smoked-meat dishes and Honey Ham.

FUKIEN STYLE

Fukien is a province on China's east coast, directly opposite Taiwan. The province has a long coastline and is noted—though not in the United States—for its fine seafood, mushroom dishes, rice-stick noodles, and excellent teas. Many dishes are light and soupy, and contain a lot of sugar. Specialties include: Clear Soup, Fermented Rice Paste, and Fish in Wine Sauce.

SHANGHAI STYLE

Shanghai, the largest city in China, is a legendary seaport at the mouth of the Yang-Tze River, where it flows into the East China Sea. Its cooking, which is representative of both the east and the central-east regions of China, tends to be somewhat well done, with more soy sauce and sugar, but without garlic, onion, or scallions. Its principal methods are red-cooking and stir-frying. Specialties include Lion's Head, Red-Cooked Pork, and Drunken Chicken.

NOTE: The recipes in this book are labeled to identify their regional sources.

HOW TO SERVE A CHINESE MEAL

The Chinese do not have knives on the table; all cutting is done in the kitchen. Diners need only chopsticks, a rice bowl, and soup spoons.

There are two different serving styles: family and banquet. The difference is in the variety and quantity of food. In family-style meals, there are but a few dishes, served at once. In banquet-style meals, the dishes are many, and served one at a time in ceremonious procession.

FAMILY STYLE

A Chinese family may have four courses for lunch or supper: meat or poultry, seafood, vegetables, and soup. All of the dishes (even the soup) are placed in the center of the table. Using chopsticks, everyone helps himself to a little of each dish, eating food and rice simultaneously. At the end of the meal, hot tea and fresh fruit are served. There is no dessert.

BANQUET STYLE

A Chinese banquet usually serves ten or twelve people around a round table, and includes about ten to eighteen dishes. Fruits and nuts are placed on the table before anyone is seated so guests can nibble until the appetizers are served. The host and hostess make a toast: "*Kan Pei!*"—which means "drink up." The guests make a return toast in appreciation of such generous hospitality, and the host then helps the guests to their food. Four hors d'oeuvres or appetizers are served. Rice is served at the beginning of the main courses, which are served one at a time. The soup is served after the main courses, and is followed by a sweet dessert. Tea is drunk before, during, and after the meal. Chinese rice wine is usually served, warm, with the hors d'oeuvres, and throughout the main courses.

Traditionally, everyone has his own bowl of rice, a plate, a spoon, and chopsticks. The dishes in the center of the table are shared; everyone eats directly from them, or the food is served from platters with serving spoons. In the modified Chinese fashion, a banquet can be served buffet style.

PLANNING YOUR OWN CHINESE MENUS

Now that you have some idea of the cooking methods and serving styles, it is not too early to begin thinking about your own menus. This section contains six sample menus to get you started. If you compare the recipes for each menu, you will begin to grasp the principles involved.

Balanced meals are important, of course, and so the sample menus draw upon the basic food groups. But more is involved. Milder dishes must be included to balance the spicy ones; and ingredients must not be repeated too often in any given meal; color is also important. Planning a Chinese meal is an art; it calls for orchestrating the individual dishes by balancing their harmonies and contrasts.

The six sample menus—three family style and three banquets—may strike you as impossibly ambitious at this moment, and rightly so. They are not there to intimidate you but to show you the heights you can achieve with practice and planning.

For now, you must learn and develop your skills. Since stir-frying requires last-minute cooking and close attention, you will not want to plan a meal that contains more than one stir-fried dish just yet. But that need not worry you. Most of the dishes in this book can easily be doubled or tripled in size. A traditional Chinese cook would accommodate a larger group by expanding the menu rather than the size of the dish, but that is an ability you can strive for in the future. Until then, you can use your planning skills to create easy-to-prepare menus. For example, there are many dishes that can be prepared in advance—cold appetizers, roasted meats, and steamed dishes—and still others that can be largely prepared ahead of time and finish-cooked just before serving.

Family Style (serves 4–6)

1. Crab Meat Rolls
   Chicken with Cashews
   Beef in Oyster Sauce
   Buddha Delight
   Hot and Sour Soup
   Boiled or Fried Rice

2. Sweet-and-Sour Meatballs
   Stir-Fried Prawns and Chicken
   Pork with Hot Pepper
   Sesame Fish
   Wonton Soup
   Boiled or Fried Rice

3. Barbecued Spareribs
   Stuffed Walnut Chicken
   Kota Beef
   Pineapple Fish
   Pork-and-Cucumber Soup
   Boiled or Fried Rice

4. Fried Wontons
   Spareribs with Salted Black Beans
   Baby Shrimp with Pine Nuts
   Stuffed Cucumber
   Tomato-Flower Soup
   Boiled or Fried Rice

Banquet Style (serves 10–12)

1. Hors d'oeuvres:
   Shrimp Toast
   Barbecued Pork
   Entrée:
   Shrimp with Cucumber Salad
   Champagne Chicken
   Tangerine-Peel Beef
   Prawns in Szechuan Sauce
   Peking Duck
   Stir-Fried Cauliflower and Mushrooms
   Yangchow Fried Rice
   Dragon-and-Phoenix Soup
   Lychee Flambé Cake

2. Hors d'oeuvres:
   Sesame-Seed Bread Rolls
   Pearl Meatballs
   Entrée:
   Bon Bon Chicken
   Scallops Canton
   Hunan Beef
   Stuffed Shrimp
   Yu Hsiang Beef
   Stir-Fried Asparagus with Pork
   Green Jade Fried Rice
   Fish-Fillet Soup
   Fried Bananas

Allow plenty of time for preparation. Plan your menu a few days—even a week or two—ahead of time. Begin by listing the dishes you want to serve, then check the ingredients called for and draw up a shopping list. It is wise to have second-choice dishes in case some ingredients for your first choice are not available. Check the cooking time for each dish, including preparation time. Make a note of when each dish should be started, and which dish should be served first. Post your menu where you can see it, so nothing is forgotten.

The most important thing is to present the food fresh, well prepared, and piping hot.

BEVERAGES

TEA

Tea has been the favorite drink of the Chinese for centuries and is inextricably woven into the fabric of Chinese life. Although tea is popular in many other countries, it seldom resembles tea as served in China. It is not difficult to learn enough so that your choice and service of tea will honor the effort you have put into cooking your Chinese meal.

The basic principles are simple. The best tea is made in a pot of china, glass, or pottery (a metal pot may give a harsh taste). Tea should be loose, not bagged. The water must not be allowed to boil too long, and it should be poured into a pot that has been rinsed in hot water.

Milk and lemon are never used; sugar only very rarely. The Chinese occasionally add flowers to their tea—jasmine flowers for jasmine tea, for example; orange flowers or chrysanthemums for green tea; and roses for red tea.

Fine tea is clear and well colored. It is fragrant and has a natural sweetness. Bad tea is too light (insufficiently steeped) or too dark (steeped too long), with a bitter taste.

The best teas are the premium whole-leaf teas and then the fine broken-leaf teas (of others we will not speak). The quality and price depend on leaf size (the smaller the better) and position on the tea plant (the leaf bud with its two adjoining leaves is much preferred).

There are four principal kinds of tea.

Unfermented or *green tea* is made from tender young leaves that have been dried in the sun or in special rooms as soon as they are picked. The leaves retain their greenish-yellow color and produce a brew that is cooling and refreshing, delicate in flavor and light in color. Some well-known varieties (not brands) of green tea include Dragon Well (Lung-Ching), considered the best in China; Gun Powder, from northern China; and Water Nymph (Sui-Sing), from Kwangtung, in southern China.

Fermented tea is also known as red tea (for its color in the cup) to the Chinese. It is produced by allowing the leaves to ferment—changing their color from green to brownish-black—before they are dried. The tea that results is rich-red, full-bodied, hearty. It is particularly good with seafood and deep-fried foods. Among the varieties of fermented tea are Keemun, one of the best and most popular; Iron Goddess of Mercy (Te Kwan Yin), which should be served in small cups, as if it were a fine brandy; and Clear Distance (Lu An), a particularly strong brew from Canton.

Semifermented tea stands between the green and black teas, and is excellent with heavy dishes and seafood. The principal variety is Oolong. Light in color but well flavored, it is produced mainly in Taiwan.

Scented tea has been blended with fresh or dried flowers; when brewed, it comes alive with fragrance. Scented teas include Jasmine (Hsiang Pien), from Fukien and Taiwan, the best-known variety; Lichee (Li Chih Cha), a faintly sweet type from Taiwan; Rose (Mei Kuei Cha), also from Taiwan; and Chrysanthemum (Chu Hwa Cha), from Chinkiang, and most unusual because it is sweetened with sugar.

When storing tea, put it in an airtight container (but never in clear glass or plastic) to prevent it from absorbing other flavors and odors. Use tea within six months for the best flavor.

WINES AND LIQUORS

There are two principal varieties of Chinese wine, white and golden. Both are made in varying strengths, and both are used in cooking and drinking, as well as for medicinal purposes. A good wine will age well, turning dark yellow and developing a thick consistency.

Chinese wine is usually served warm, in very small cups. The warming can speed intoxication, thus the small cups and the practice of always taking some food with the wine. In traditional Chinese social life, there is no counterpart to the Western cocktail party; at parties, the food is always paramount and the drinks merely adjuncts.

In cooking, the alcohol evaporates, leaving only the wine's flavor behind. Small amounts of wine are often added to dishes to blend flavors and neutralize odors. Many marinades require wine in generous quantities.

Chinese wines and liquors are hard to find in the U.S., but they are worth looking for in Oriental markets. If you are unable to find them, keep in mind that dry sherry is a useful substitute for rice wine, which is called Shao-Hsing. It is amber in color and mild. Other Chinese wines are named for the fruits from which they are made: lychee, plum, pear, and orange.

Chinese liquors are potent. Some important varieties include Ng Ga Pay, flavored with herbs; Kaoliang, distilled from sorghum grain; Mao-Tai, also from sorghum, and very strong; Pai-Kan, from corn; and Mei Kwei Lu, which is flavored with rose petals, but not sweet.

Almost any red or white wine made from grapes will go well with Chinese dishes, and beer is a good choice for hearty foods.

✻ RECIPES ✻

PREPARED INGREDIENTS

Toasted Sesame Seeds

Toast ½ cup sesame seeds in a dry wok or saucepan over medium heat. Stir constantly until seeds turn light brown. Remove and let cool. Store in air-tight jar.

Crushed Toasted Sesame Seeds

Crush ½ cup toasted sesame seeds in a blender for a few seconds. Store in air-tight jar. Will keep for about one month, refrigerated.

Sesame-Seed Paste

½ cup toasted sesame seeds
¼ cup sesame oil

Pour oil and seeds into blender and whip into a paste. Store in air-tight jar. Will keep several months refrigerated.

Szechuan Peppercorn Powder

Heat ¼ cup Szechuan peppercorns in a dry wok or saucepan over low heat 4–5 minutes, stirring constantly, until they begin to smoke. Cool and crush with a mortar and pestle or blender. Store in air-tight jar. Will keep a few months refrigerated.

Szechuan Peppercorn Salt

¼ cup Szechuan peppercorns
2 tablespoons salt

Heat Szechuan peppercorns and salt in a dry wok or a saucepan over low heat for 2–3 minutes. Remove and let cool. Crush them in a blender or with a mortar and pestle. Store in glass jar. Szechuan Peppercorn Salt will keep for a few months without refrigeration.

Blanched Walnuts

2 cups walnuts
4 cups water

Bring 4 cups of water to a boil in medium saucepan. Add walnuts and blanch them for ½ minute. (Blanching removes the bitter taste from the skin.) Drain and spread walnuts on paper towels. Let them dry overnight or in 150-degree oven for ½ hour. Store in refrigerator in plastic bags.

Fried Nuts

1 cup almonds, cashews, peanuts, pine nuts, or walnuts
1½ cups salad oil

Heat the oil in a wok or saucepan over medium low heat. When oil becomes warm, add nuts. Fold and stir constantly until nuts turn light brown. (Do not overcook the nuts and do not allow oil to become hot—nuts are easy to burn.) Store nuts in plastic bag or glass jar.

Fried Shrimp Chips

¼ pound dried shrimp chips
Peanut or other salad oil for frying

Heat 2–3 inches of oil in a wok or a deep-fryer to 400 degrees. (Test with one shrimp chip: If it puffs in 5 seconds, oil is ready.) Fry chips a few at a time until they puff. Drain and store in plastic bags when cool. Will keep about 2 weeks.

MANDARIN PANCAKES
PO PING ■ National

薄　餅

1 cup sifted all-purpose flour
⅓ cup boiling water
2 tablespoons cold water
2 tablespoons peanut or other salad oil
All-purpose flour for dusting

1. Stir sifted flour into boiling water. Cool no more than 5 minutes; knead warm dough with cold water until smooth. Let stand 30 minutes, covered.

2. Knead again on a lightly floured surface about 2 minutes until smooth and elastic. Shape into a roll about 1-inch in diameter and cut into 1-inch pieces (a). Dust lightly with flour and flatten pieces to about ½-inch thick (b).

3. Brush tops with oil and dust again (c). Gently press two pancakes together, joining oiled sides.

4. Lightly dust unoiled surfaces with flour. With a rolling pin, roll each pair gently into paper-thin pancakes about 6 inches in diameter (d).

5. Heat an ungreased skillet over low heat. Cook pancakes one pair at a time 30 seconds on each side until transparent, bubbly in center, and very lightly brown (e). Gently peel the two pancakes apart while still warm (f). Cover with damp cloth until ready to serve.

NOTE: Mandarin pancakes can also be bought in Chinese stores.

TO PREPARE AHEAD: Follow steps 1–5 and freeze. Before serving, thaw and steam 5 minutes a dozen at a time, or wrap in foil, then wrap in wet dish towel and reheat 30 minutes in a 250-degree oven.

Makes 1 dozen

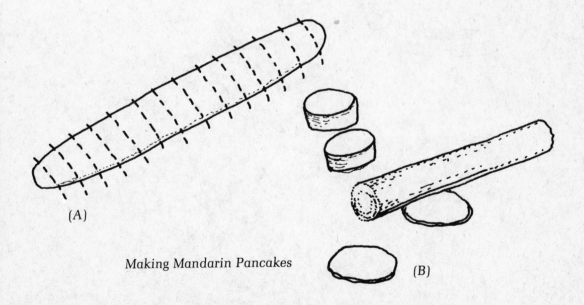

(A)

Making Mandarin Pancakes

(B)

43

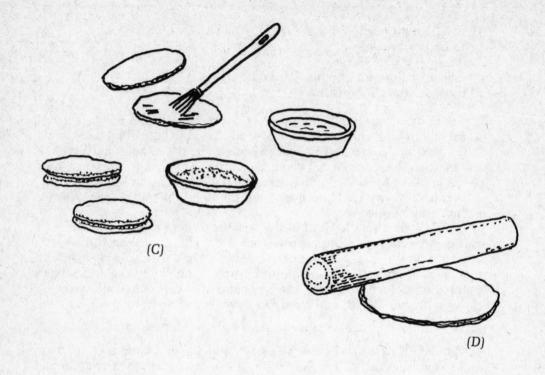

(C)

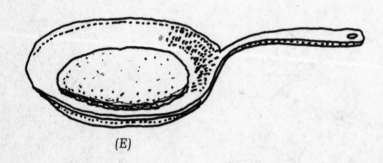

(D)

(E)

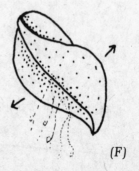

(F)

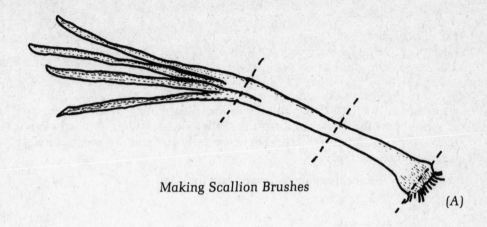

Making Scallion Brushes

(A)

Scallion Brushes

Wash and trim the scallions. Remove roots and green stems. Cut into 2-inch lengths (a).

With the tip of a sharp paring knife, cut ends lengthwise, making ½-inch slashes close together (b). Soak in ice water 30 minutes or more until ends curl back (c).

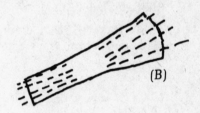

(B)

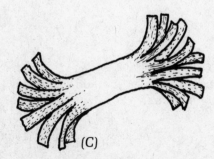

(C)

EGG SKINS
TAN P'I ■ National

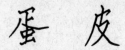

4 eggs
¼ teaspoon salt
Dash of white pepper
2 tablespoons peanut or other salad oil

1. Mix the eggs, salt, and pepper.
2. Heat an oiled 10-inch skillet over low heat. Pour ¼ of the egg mixture at a time into the skillet and tip the skillet side-to-side to spread evenly. Cook over low heat until set; turn over carefully and cook 10 seconds longer. Remove in one piece.

NOTE: May be kept frozen in a plastic bag for a few weeks.

Makes 4 skins

CHICKEN STOCK
GEE T'ANG ■ National

1 stewing chicken, 4–5 pounds, or 5 pounds chicken backs or necks
4 slices fresh ginger
2 whole scallions, cut in half, including stems
1 whole star anise
3 quarts water
½ cup rice wine or dry sherry

1. Wash chicken thoroughly.
2. Put chicken, ginger, scallions, star anise, water, and rice wine in a large heavy pot and bring to a boil. Reduce heat to medium-low; cover and cook 2 hours or until chicken is tender and the liquid is reduced to half.
3. Remove chicken and strain stock; allow to cool, and refrigerate.
4. Skim fat before using.

TO PREPARE AHEAD: 1. Pour stock into ice-cube trays and freeze. 2. Remove the cubes from trays and put in plastic bags.

Makes 2 quarts

Ginger Sherry

This is the best way to store fresh ginger.

¼ pound fresh ginger
1 cup rice wine or dry sherry

Peel ginger; wash, dry, and slice. Place ginger in a jar and add sherry to cover. Will keep in refrigerator 1 week to 6 months.

Makes 1½ cups

HORS D'OEUVRES AND APPETIZERS

BARBECUED PORK
CH'A SHAO ▪ Canton

2 pounds boneless pork loin or fresh ham, well trimmed
¼ cup honey

MARINADE:
½ cup soy sauce
¼ cup rice wine or dry sherry
1 tablespoon packed brown sugar
1 tablespoon commercial hoisin sauce
½ teaspoon salt
1 teaspoon sesame-seed oil
2 cloves garlic, chopped
Dash of pepper

1. Cut the pork with the grain into slices 1½ inches thick. Cut the slices into strips 2 inches wide, ¼-inch deep on all sides at 1-inch intervals.

2. Combine marinade and mix thoroughly. Add pork and toss to coat well. Cover and marinate in refrigerator for 2–3 hours or overnight, turning occasionally.

3. Preheat oven to 300 degrees. Line a baking pan with foil and add ½-inch hot water. Place the pork on a rack and roast 30 minutes on each side or until light brown.

4. Raise heat to 400 degrees. Brush honey thickly on all sides of pork and roast 5–10 minutes longer.

5. Slice barbecued pork against the grain into slices ⅛-inch thick. Serve hot or at room temperature. This dish is also perfect for sandwiches and can be stir-fried with any vegetable as a main course.

NOTE: 1. Pork can also be barbecued over low heat.
2. Leftovers can be frozen. To serve, thaw, baste again with honey, and reheat at 400 degrees for 8–10 minutes.

TO PREPARE AHEAD: Follow steps 1–3 two days before serving and refrigerate the pork in a plastic bag. Resume cooking at your convenience.

Makes 4 servings

CRAB MEAT ROLLS
PANG HSIEH CHUAN ▪ National

4 dozen wonton wrappers, 3″ × 3″
1 cup plum sauce (page 64)
¼ cup mustard sauce (page 63)

FILLING:
2 tablespoons peanut or other salad oil for stir-frying
½ pound fresh or canned crab meat (regular, not lump) or minced shrimp or veal
1 cup chopped celery
1 cup shredded water chestnuts
½ cup shredded bamboo shoots
3 scallions, chopped, including stems
¼ teaspoon salt
1 teaspoon sesame-seed oil
2 tablespoons rice wine or dry sherry
Dash of white pepper
1 tablespoon cornstarch dissolved in 3 tablespoons cold water

1. Cover wonton wrappers with damp cloth; prepare the plum sauce and mustard sauce.
2. Flake crab meat, removing cartilage.

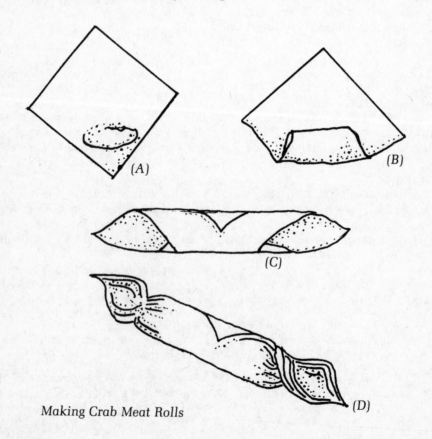

Making Crab Meat Rolls

3. Heat oil in a wok or skillet over high heat. Add celery, water chestnuts, and bamboo shoots. Stir-fry 1 minute. Add crab meat, scallions, salt, sesame-seed oil, sherry, and white pepper. Stir-fry 30 seconds. Stir in dissolved cornstarch and stir constantly until sauce thickens. Allow to cool.

4. Place 1 teaspoon filling about an inch from one corner of a moistened wonton wrapper (a). Fold corner over filling (b) and roll wrapper into a cylinder (c). Insert a finger into each end and twist the tube to seal (d). (The filling may also be used cold as a cocktail spread.)

5. Heat 2–3 inches of oil in a wok or deep-fryer to 375 degrees. Fry rolls 2–3 minutes, until golden brown. Serve hot with plum sauce and mustard sauce.

TO PREPARE AHEAD: Follow steps 1–5 up to 2 weeks ahead and freeze in a plastic bag. Before serving, place unthawed rolls on a rack in a preheated oven for 15 to 20 minutes at 375 degrees.

Makes 4 dozen

FRIED WONTON
CHA HUN TUN ▪ National

炸 餛 飩

40 wonton wrappers, 3″ × 3″
Plum sauce (page 64)
Mustard sauce (page 63)
Peanut or other salad oil for deep-frying

FILLING:
½ pound ground chuck (or veal or chicken or shrimp)
¼ cup minced water chestnuts
1 tablespoon soy sauce
1 tablespoon rice wine or dry sherry
¾ teaspoon salt
¼ teaspoon sugar
1 teaspoon sesame-seed oil
1 egg
2 scallions, minced, including stems
Dash of pepper

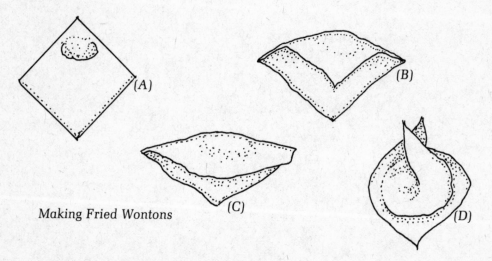

Making Fried Wontons

1. Prepare the plum sauce and mustard sauce.
2. Combine filling ingredients in mixing bowl and mix well.
3. Cover wonton wrappers with damp cloth. Place ½ teaspoon filling in one corner of each moistened side (a). Fold one corner ⅓ over to cover meat (b). Roll folded corner over once (c). Wet two unjoined corners and join (d); press together. Make wontons one at a time, keeping remaining wrappers under cloth so they don't dry out.
4. Heat 2 inches of oil to 350 degrees in a wok, or 3 inches of oil in deep-fryer. Fry wontons, turning constantly, for 2–3 minutes or until golden brown. Drain on paper towels. Serve hot with plum sauce and mustard sauce.

TO PREPARE AHEAD: Follow steps 1–4 and freeze wontons in a plastic bag. Before serving, bake unthawed wontons on a rack 8–10 minutes in a pre-heated oven at 375 degrees until crispy and golden brown.

Makes 3 dozen

SHRIMP TOAST
HSIA JEN TU SSU ▪ Peking

蝦仁吐司

8 slices two-day-old bread
Peanut or other salad oil for deep-frying

FILLING:
½ pound shrimp, shelled, deveined, and washed
¼ pound ground beef
2 tablespoons minced water chestnuts
1 scallion, minced, including stems
½ teaspoon salt
⅛ teaspoon white pepper
2 teaspoons sesame-seed oil or other salad oil
1 tablespoon rice wine or dry sherry
½ teaspoon sugar
1 medium egg
2 teaspoons cornstarch dissolved in 1 tablespoon cold water

1. Trim crusts and cut each bread slice into four triangles. (Fresh bread can be dried in a warm oven about 30 minutes or dried at room temperature about 12 hours.)

2. Dry shrimp thoroughly with paper towels and grind them in a grinder or blender. Combine with remaining filling ingredients and mix well.

3. Spread 1 teaspoon filling on each triangle.

4. Heat 2 inches of oil in wok or 3 inches of oil in deep-fryer to 375 degrees. Add shrimp toast, filling side down, and fry golden brown on both sides. Drain on paper towels. Serve hot.

TO PREPARE AHEAD: Follow steps 1–4, frying to light brown only, and freeze triangles in plastic bags. Before serving, bake unthawed toast on a rack in a preheated 375-degree oven 10–15 minutes until crispy and golden brown.

Makes 32 Shrimp Toasts

CHINESE CORN BREAD
YU MI KAO ▪ National

3 cups cornbread mix
1 cup milk
3 eggs
½ cup peanut or other salad oil
1½ cups chopped onion
2 cups canned creamed corn
2 fresh or dried hot peppers, minced
½ cup chopped cooked ham
4 slices bacon, fried crisp and crumbled
½ teaspoon salt
2 cloves garlic, minced
½ teaspoon white pepper

1. Mix the cornbread mix, milk, eggs, and oil; beat well. Add remaining ingredients and mix well. Pour into a well-greased 9×12-inch cake pan and bake in a preheated oven for 30–35 minutes at 400 degrees until golden brown. Cool 10 minutes and cut into squares. Serve hot or warm.

TO PREPARE AHEAD: Make cornbread up to 2 weeks ahead. Cover and freeze. Before serving, thaw and reheat 10–15 minutes at 375 degrees.

Makes 8–10 servings

BARBECUED PEANUT CHICKEN WINGS
KAO GEE TZU ▪ Canton

烤鷄翅

12 chicken wings
⅔ cup chopped raw peanuts
½ pound bacon, sliced thin

MARINADE:
½ cup soy sauce
¼ cup rice wine or dry sherry
2 tablespoons brown sugar, packed
1 tablespoon honey
1 tablespoon commercial hoisin sauce
1 tablespoon tomato paste
1 clove garlic, minced
¼ teaspoon white pepper

1. Remove wing tips and cut wings in two pieces at the joint.
2. Combine marinade; add wings, chill and marinate 6 hours or overnight.
3. Add bacon and marinate 5 minutes.
4. Coat wings with peanuts and wrap with bacon.
5. Arrange wings on a rack in a foil-lined roasting pan. Bake in a preheated oven 20–30 minutes at 375 degrees, until golden brown and crispy. Serve hot.

TO PREPARE AHEAD: Follow steps 1–4 the day before and refrigerate. Before serving, follow step 5.

Makes 12

BARBECUED SPARERIBS
K'AO P'AI KU ▪ Canton

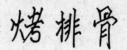

½ cup plum sauce (page 64)
2 racks pork spareribs (about 5 pounds)
⅓ cup honey

MARINADE:
2 cloves garlic, crushed
2 thin slices fresh ginger
1 scallion, including stems, cut into 2-inch pieces
½ cup soy sauce
½ cup rice wine or dry sherry
2 tablespoons brown sugar, packed
2 tablespoons commercial hoisin sauce
1 tablespoon tomato paste
½ teaspoon salt
Dash of pepper

1. Prepare plum sauce.
2. Mix the marinade well and pour over ribs in a roasting pan; cover with foil.
3. Bake for 30 minutes on each side at 300 degrees. Drain.
4. Brush ribs generously with honey on both sides.
5. Oven-roast on a rack 10–15 minutes on each side at 450 degrees or grill over charcoal. Cut into individual ribs and serve with plum sauce.

TO PREPARE AHEAD: Follow steps 1–3; cover and refrigerate. Before serving, follow steps 4 and 5.

Makes 4 servings

BUTTERFLY SHRIMP
HU TIEH HSIA ■ Canton

蝴蝶蝦

½ cup apricot sauce (page 63)
2 ounces fried shrimp chips (page 42)
1 pound large shrimp (25–30)
1 teaspoon fresh lemon juice
1 tablespoon rice wine or dry sherry
1 tablespoon salt
1 tablespoon honey
Flour for coating
Peanut or other salad oil for deep-frying

BATTER A:
½ cup beer or white wine
¼ cup cornstarch
¼ cup flour
3½ tablespoons sweet rice flour
⅔ teaspoon baking powder
⅔ teaspoon salt
¼ teaspoon garlic powder
¼ teaspoon soy sauce

BATTER B:
⅓ cup beer
1 egg
½ cup flour
2 tablespoons cornstarch
¼ teaspoon baking powder
¼ teaspoon garlic powder
½ teaspoon salt
Dash of white pepper

Making Butterfly Shrimp

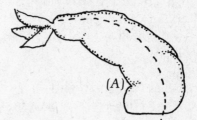

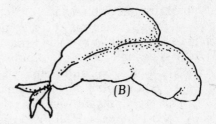

1. Prepare apricot sauce and shrimp chips.
2. Shell and devein the shrimp, leaving tails intact. Wash and pat dry. Split lengthwise (a), but do not cut all the way through (b).
3. Combine lemon juice, sherry, salt, and honey; mix well and toss with shrimp. Let stand 10 minutes. Toss shrimp with flour in a plastic bag to coat; shake off excess flour.
4. No more than a few minutes ahead of time, mix Batter A or Batter B, making sure it is free of lumps.
5. Heat 2 inches of oil in a wok or 3 inches of oil in a deep-fryer to 375 degrees. Dip shrimp in batter by the tail and fry until light brown. Drain; serve immediately with apricot sauce and shrimp chips.

TO PREPARE AHEAD: Only a few hours ahead of time, follow steps 1–5, frying to pale brown only. Refrigerate. Re-fry before serving.

Makes 4 servings

CRISPY SHRIMP BALLS
TS'UI P'I HSIA CHIU ▪ Canton

脆皮蝦球

1 cup ginger sauce (page 64)
1 pound small shrimp, shelled and deveined
¼ pound ground beef
1 teaspoon minced fresh ginger
2 scallions, minced, including stems
2 tablespoons minced water chestnuts
1½ teaspoons salt
2 teaspoons sesame-seed oil
1 tablespoon rice wine or dry sherry
1 egg
2 tablespoons cornstarch dissolved in 3 tablespoons cold water
Dash of white pepper
Peanut or other salad oil for deep-frying

COATING:
1 egg
1 tablespoon all-purpose flour
4 ounces rice sticks, broken into 1-inch pieces

1. Rub the shrimp with 1 teaspoon salt. Rinse; squeeze dry and grind in meat grinder or blender.
2. Combine shrimp, beef, minced ginger, scallions, water chestnuts, remaining salt, sesame-seed oil, rice wine, egg, dissolved cornstarch, and white pepper; mix for 5 minutes, cover and chill 30 minutes.
3. Combine egg and flour; mix until free of lumps.
4. Form mixture into 1-inch balls; dip in egg-and-flour mixture and shake off excess. Roll gently in rice sticks, cover completely.
5. Heat 3 inches of oil to 400 degrees in a wok or deep-fryer. Fry balls two at a time only for about 15 seconds. The rice sticks should be puffed up, white, and crispy. Drain.
6. Bake for 15 minutes at 350 degrees. Serve immediately with ginger sauce.

TO PREPARE AHEAD: Follow steps 1–5 and refrigerate. Before serving, follow step 6.

Makes 3 dozen

EGG ROLLS
CH'UN CHUAN ▪ National

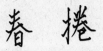

16 egg-roll wrappers
1 cup plum sauce (page 64)
¼ cup mustard sauce (page 63)
1 egg, well beaten
Peanut or other salad oil for deep-frying

MARINADE:
1 tablespoon cornstarch
1 teaspoon salt
1 tablespoon rice wine or dry sherry

FILLING:
5 tablespoons peanut or other salad oil
½ pound small shrimp, shelled, deveined, washed, and patted dry
¼ pound ground chuck
5 cups thinly sliced Chinese cabbage
½ cup shredded water chestnuts
½ cup shredded bamboo shoots
1 pound fresh bean sprouts, rinsed with cold water and well drained
1 scallion, chopped
1 teaspoon sesame-seed oil
3 tablespoons soy sauce
1 tablespoon rice wine or dry sherry
1 teaspoon salt
1 teaspoon sugar
Dash of pepper
2 tablespoons cornstarch dissolved in 2 tablespoons cold water

1. Prepare plum sauce and mustard sauce.
2. Mix marinade and marinate shrimp for 10 minutes.
3. Heat 3 tablespoons of oil in a wok or skillet until very hot; stir-fry shrimp 30 seconds. Remove and set aside.
4. Stir-fry ground chuck 1 minute in 1 tablespoon of oil. Remove and set aside.
5. Stir-fry cabbage, water chestnuts, bamboo shoots, bean sprouts, and scallion 1 minute in 1 tablespoon of oil. Add sesame-seed oil, soy sauce, sherry, salt, sugar, and pepper; stir-fry 1 minute longer. Add shrimp and ground chuck; mix well. Stir in dissolved cornstarch. Cook, stirring constantly, until sauce thickens. Turn into large colander, press gently, and drain well. Allow to cool.

6. Place 2 tablespoons filling on lower half of egg roll wrapper (a). Use a pastry brush to moisten all edges of wrapper with egg. Fold the bottom edge up (b), then fold the left and right edges over (c). Roll until completely folded (d, e).

7. Heat 2–3 inches of oil to 375 degrees in a wok or deep-fryer. Add egg rolls 4 or 5 at a time, seam-side down. Fry, turning constantly, until golden brown and crispy. Serve hot with plum sauce and mustard sauce.

NOTE: 1. Two tablespoons of cornstarch dissolved in $\frac{1}{4}$ cup cold water can be used to seal egg rolls.
2. Any combination of meat and seafood can be used.
3. In order to make crispy egg rolls, the filling should be drained well and cooled.

TO PREPARE AHEAD: Follow steps 1–7, frying to *light* brown only. Freeze in plastic bags in single layers. Before serving, reheat frozen egg rolls on rack in a preheated 375-degree oven 20–30 minutes until crispy, or re-fry until golden brown.

Makes 16 egg rolls

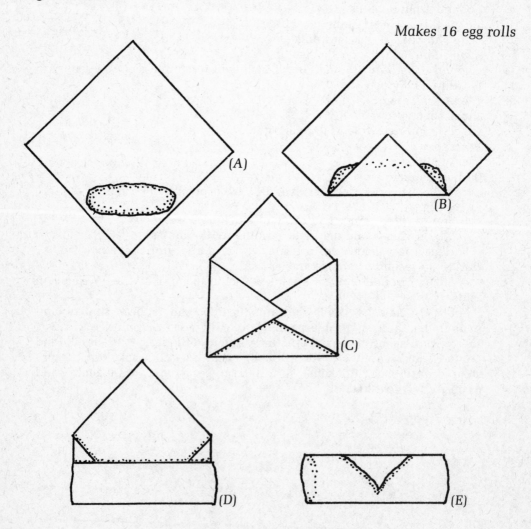

Making Egg Rolls

PEARL MEATBALLS
CHEN CHU ROW WAN ▪ Hunan

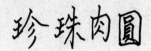

¼ cup hot pepper sauce dip (page 62)
1 cup glutinous rice (sweet rice)
1 pound ground pork or veal
2 tablespoons minced water chestnuts
2 tablespoons minced cooked ham
1 scallion, minced, including stems
1 tablespoon soy sauce
½ teaspoon salt
½ teaspoon sugar
2 tablespoons rice wine or dry sherry
1 egg
1 tablespoon cornstarch dissolved in 2 tablespoons cold water
1 teaspoon sesame-seed oil

1. Prepare hot pepper sauce dip.
2. Wash the rice in cold water; soak in 3 cups cold water overnight.
3. Combine ground meat, water chestnuts, ham, scallion, soy sauce, salt, sugar, rice wine, egg, dissolved cornstarch, and sesame-seed oil and mix well. Cover and chill 20 minutes.
4. Drain rice well. Make 1-teaspoon balls of meat mixture and roll in rice until well covered.
5. Arrange the meatballs a half-inch apart on a platter. Steam 45 minutes and serve hot.

TO PREPARE AHEAD: Follow steps 1–5 but steam only 30 minutes, and refrigerate. Before serving, steam 15 minutes.

Makes 2½ dozen

SESAME-SEED BREAD ROLLS
CHIH MA MIEN PAO CHUAN ▪ Canton

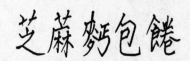

12 slices fresh white bread
1 egg, well beaten
¼ cup sesame seeds
Peanut or other salad oil for deep-frying

FILLING:
1 tablespoon peanut or other salad oil
½ cup minced onion
4 ounces ground beef
4 ounces shrimp, shelled, deveined, washed, and chopped
1 tablespoon soy sauce
1 tablespoon rice wine or dry sherry
½ teaspoon salt
Dash of white pepper
1 tablespoon cornstarch dissolved in 2 tablespoons cold water

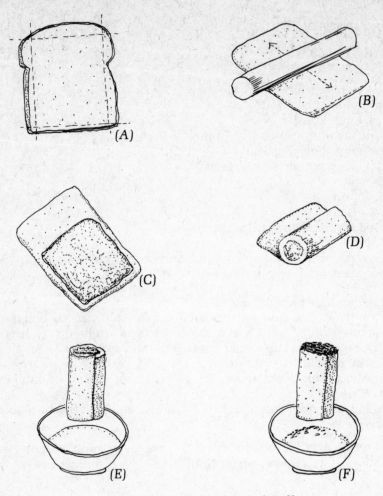

Making Sesame-Seed Bread Rolls

1. Trim the crusts off the bread (a). Lightly flatten bread into thin slices with rolling pin (b).

2. Heat 1 tablespoon of oil in a wok or skillet over high heat. Stir-fry onion 1 minute until transparent. Add beef; stir-fry 30 seconds. Add shrimp, soy sauce, sherry, salt, and white pepper; stir in dissolved cornstarch. Stir constantly until sauce thickens and boils. Remove and allow to cool.

3. Spread a thin layer of filling on two-thirds of each slice of bread, leaving a half-inch margin at the edge (c). Brush edges with beaten egg and roll up slices, starting at the filled end (d).

4. Dip both ends in beaten egg, then in sesame seeds (e, f).

5. Heat 1 inch of oil in wok or deep-fryer to 375 degrees. Add bread rolls, seam-side down, and fry golden brown on all sides. Drain, cut in half crosswise and serve hot.

TO PREPARE AHEAD: Follow steps 1–5, frying to light brown only; freeze in plastic bag. Before serving, bake frozen rolls on a rack in a preheated oven 15–20 minutes at 350 degrees.

Makes 1 dozen (4 servings)

SWEET-AND-SOUR MEATBALLS
T'IEN SUAN RUH WAN ▪ Canton

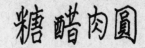

MEAT BALLS:
  1 pound ground chuck or pork
  2 tablespoons soy sauce
  2 tablespoons rice wine or dry sherry
  ½ teaspoon salt
  1 egg
  1 tablespoon cornstarch dissolved in 4 tablespoons cold water
  2 scallions, minced, including stems
  Dash of pepper
  Peanut or other salad oil for deep-frying

SWEET-AND-SOUR SAUCE:
  ⅔ cup plum preserves
  1 clove garlic, minced
  ⅓ cup sugar
  ⅓ cup cider vinegar
  ¾ cup water

  1. Combine meatball ingredients and mix well. Roll into 1-inch balls.
  2. Heat 2 inches of oil in a wok or deep-fryer to 375 degrees. Fry meatballs until golden brown. Drain.
  3. Combine sauce ingredients in a saucepan; bring to a boil.
  4. Add meatballs, cooking over medium heat for 20 minutes and stirring occasionally. Serve hot with toothpicks.

TO PREPARE AHEAD: Follow steps 1–3 and refrigerate or freeze in sauce, depending on storage time. If frozen, thaw two hours. Cook in sauce 25 minutes.

Makes 2½ dozen

DIPPING SAUCES 調味料

Hot Pepper Oil

⅓ cup peanut oil
⅓ cup sesame-seed oil
⅓ cup crushed hot chili peppers

Heat the peanut and sesame oil in a saucepan over medium heat; fry peppers until dark brown. Allow to cool.

NOTE: Hot pepper oil can be purchased in an Oriental grocery store.

Hot Pepper Sauce Dip

¼ cup soy sauce
1 tablespoon cider vinegar
1 tablespoon sugar
1 tablespoon sesame-seed oil
1 teaspoon hot chili paste

Mix the ingredients and store in jar. Keeps in refrigerator at least one month.

Hot Pepper Oil Dip

1 tablespoon sugar
1 tablespoon vinegar
3 tablespoons soy sauce
1½ teaspoons hot pepper oil
1 scallion, minced, including stems

Mix the ingredients and store in jar. Keeps in refrigerator a few days.

Spicy Hoisin Sauce Dip

1 teaspoon sugar
1 tablespoon vinegar
3 tablespoons soy sauce
1 tablespoon commercial hoisin sauce
1 teaspoon hot pepper oil

Mix the ingredients and store in jar. Keeps in refrigerator a few weeks.

Hoisin Sauce Dip

2 tablespoons commercial hoisin sauce
1 tablespoon honey
1 tablespoon soy sauce

Mix ingredients and store in jar. Keeps a few months in refrigerator.

Spicy Apricot Sauce

1½ cups apricot preserve
3 tablespoons tomato paste
1 tablespoon hot chili sauce or paste
¼ cup sugar
½ cup water
1 tablespoon cornstarch dissolved in 3 tablespoons cold water

Mix ingredients except cornstarch and cook over medium low heat for 5 minutes until well blended. Add dissolved cornstarch, stirring constantly until sauce thickens. Remove and allow to let cool. Serve with hors d'oeuvres or appetizer. Keeps 2 weeks in refrigerator.

Mustard Sauce

2 tablespoons Chinese powdered mustard
3 tablespoons boiling water
1 tablespoon vinegar
1 teaspoon sugar

Pour boiling water a little at a time into mustard; stir vigorously until smooth. Add vinegar and sugar and mix well. Cover and chill 2–3 hours to develop flavor.

Makes ⅓ cup

Apricot Sauce

½ cup apricot preserves
⅓ cup cider vinegar
2 tablespoons honey
2 tablespoons commercial hoisin sauce
½ teaspoon paprika

Mix the apricot preserves, vinegar, honey, hoisin sauce, and paprika and cook 10–15 minutes over low heat. Store in sterilized jar in refrigerator.

Makes 1 cup

Ginger Sauce

⅔ cup apricot preserves
½ cup plum sauce (see below)
¼ cup chopped crystallized ginger
2 dried chili peppers, chopped
1 cup cider vinegar
2 tablespoons honey

Mix ingredients and cook 10–15 minutes over low heat. Store in a sterilized jar in refrigerator for up to 2 months.

Makes 2 cups

Plum Sauce (Duck Sauce)

1 cup red plum preserves
½ cup apricot preserves
2 tablespoons honey
⅔ cup cider vinegar
1 clove garlic, minced

Mix ingredients in a saucepan; bring to a boil over medium heat. Cook 5 minutes, stirring constantly. Store in sterilized jar in refrigerator.

Makes 2½ cups

Orange Sauce

1 cup orange marmalade
1 tablespoon chopped crystallized ginger
⅓ cup cider vinegar
2 tablespoons rice wine or dry sherry
2 tablespoons soy sauce
½ cup orange juice

Mix ingredients and cook over medium heat, stirring constantly. Store in sterilized jar in refrigerator.

Makes 2 cups

MEAT

猪牛肉

BAMBOO-SKEWERED BEEF
CHU CH'UAN NIU NUH ▪ Canton

竹串肉

1 pound beef tenderloin or sirloin steak
12 ounces fresh mushrooms
2 dozen bamboo or metal skewers

MARINADE:
¼ cup soy sauce
¼ teaspoon salt
1 tablespoon sugar
1 tablespoon honey
2 tablespoons kaoling or gin
1 teaspoon sesame-seed or other salad oil
1 clove garlic, minced
½ tablespoon minced fresh ginger
2 tablespoons toasted sesame seeds
Dash of white pepper

1. Slice the beef ⅓-inch thick and cut into 1-inch squares.
2. Mix marinade ingredients well; add beef and toss to coat well. Marinate 15 minutes. Add mushrooms; marinate additional 15 minutes. Spear beef and mushrooms alternately on skewers, about ½-inch apart.
3. Grill over charcoal or broil in oven about 2 minutes; turn and broil 2 minutes longer. Do not overcook; beef should be tender and juicy. Serve immediately; do not delay this dish.

NOTE: 1. Before using bamboo skewers, soak in water 5 minutes to prevent burning.
2. This dish may be cooked on a small hibachi, with each guest cooking to his own taste.
3. Veal, shrimp, or scallops may be used instead of beef.

TO PREPARE AHEAD: Follow steps 1–2; cover and refrigerate, reserving marinade. Before serving, brush with marinade and broil over charcoal or in oven 3 minutes each side.

Makes 4 servings

BEEF IN HOISIN SAUCE
HAI SIEN CHIANG NIU RUH ▪ Canton

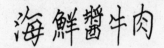

1 pound sirloin tip
1 pound onions
6 tablespoons peanut or other salad oil
1 tablespoon soy sauce
1 teaspoon salt

MARINADE:
2 tablespoons soy sauce
2 tablespoons rice wine or dry sherry
¼ teaspoon baking soda
½ teaspoon salt
½ teaspoon sugar
1 teaspoon sesame-seed oil
2 teaspoons cornstarch dissolved in 3 tablespoons cold water
Dash of pepper

HOISIN SAUCE:
1 tablespoon commercial hoisin sauce
1 teaspoon salt
1 cup beef or chicken broth
1 tablespoon cornstarch dissolved in 2 tablespoons cold water

1. Slice the beef against grain, ⅛-inch thick and julienne into 2-inch lengths.
2. Combine marinade ingredients and mix well. Add beef, toss to coat. Cover and chill 2 hours minimum.
3. Add 1 tablespoon oil to beef and mix well in order to separate each piece of meat.
4. Skin and cut ends off onions; split lengthwise; slice halves thin crosswise.
5. Heat 4 tablespoons of oil in a wok or skillet until very hot. Stir-fry beef 1 minute and set aside.
6. Heat remaining tablespoon of oil over high heat. Stir-fry onions 1 minute. Add soy sauce and salt; fry for 30 seconds longer. Return beef to wok, mixing well. Transfer to a heated serving plate and hold in a warm oven. (Alternatively, the dish may be served as is, without hoisin sauce.)
7. Combine all sauce ingredients in a small saucepan over low heat. Cook, stirring constantly until sauce thickens and boils. Pour over beef and serve hot.

TO PREPARE AHEAD: Follow step 1 and freeze. The day before serving, thaw beef and follow steps 2 and 3; refrigerate. Before serving, follow steps 4–7.

Makes 2–4 servings

BEEF IN OYSTER SAUCE
HAO YU NIU RUH ▪ Canton

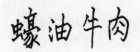

   1 pound sirloin tip
   1 tablespoon peanut, or other salad oil
   ½ cup peanut or other salad oil
   ½ pound fresh snow peas
   1 cup sliced bamboo shoots
   1 cup sliced water chestnuts
   1 scallion, chopped, including stems

MARINADE:
   1 tablespoon cornstarch dissolved in ¼ cup water
   2 tablespoons soy sauce
   1 tablespoon rice wine or dry sherry
   ½ teaspoon salt
   1 teaspoon sugar
   ½ teaspoon baking soda
   1 teaspoon sesame-seed oil

SEASONING SAUCE:
   1 tablespoon soy sauce
   1 tablespoon oyster sauce
   ½ teaspoon salt
   ½ cup chicken broth
   1½ teaspoons cornstarch dissolved in 2 tablespoons cold water

   1. Slice the beef against the grain into ⅛-inch thick; cut slices into 1½ × 2 inches.
   2. Mix marinade ingredients; add beef and toss to coat. Cover and chill 2 hours minimum.
   3. Add 1 tablespoon oil to beef mixture and mix well in order to separate each piece of meat.
   4. Mix seasoning sauce and set aside.
   5. Heat ½ cup oil in a wok or skillet until very hot. Stir-fry beef 1 minute; drain well. Reserve oil.
   6. Heat 2 tablespoons reserved oil in a wok or skillet over high heat. Add snow peas, bamboo shoots, water chestnuts, and scallion; stir-fry 1 minute. Blend in seasoning sauce and stir constantly, until it thickens and boils. Return beef to wok and mix well. Serve immediately.

TO PREPARE AHEAD: Follow step 1 and freeze. The day before serving, thaw and follow step 2. To complete, follow steps 3–6.

Makes 2–4 servings

HUNAN BEEF
HUNAN NIU LIU ▪ Hunan

湖南牛柳

1 pound beef fillet or flank steak
2 tablespoons peanut or other salad oil
4 cups bite-sized pieces of cut broccoli florets
½ cup peanut or other salad oil
½ teaspoon salt
¼ cup chicken broth

MARINADE:
1 tablespoon cornstarch dissolved in ¼ cup cold water
1 tablespoon rice wine or dry sherry
2 tablespoons soy sauce
¼ teaspoon baking soda
½ teaspoon salt
½ teaspoon sugar

HUNAN SAUCE:
1 tablespoon peanut or other salad oil
2 cloves garlic, minced
1 teaspoon minced fresh ginger
2 dried chili peppers, chopped
¾ cup chicken broth
3 tablespoons soy sauce
1 teaspoon cider vinegar
½ teaspoon salt
1 teaspoon sugar
1⅓ tablespoons cornstarch dissolved in 3 tablespoons cold water

1. Slice beef ¼-inch thick, then cut slices into 1″ × 2″ pieces.
2. Mix marinade; add beef and toss to coat. Cover and chill 90 minutes minimum.
3. Add 2 tablespoons oil to beef; mix well to separate pieces.
4. Wash broccoli florets and drain well.
5. Heat ½ cup oil in a wok or skillet until very hot. Stir-fry beef for 1 minute. Remove, drain and transfer to warm oven. Reserve oil.
6. Heat 1 tablespoon of oil in a wok or skillet over high heat and stir-fry salt, broccoli, and ¼ cup chicken broth 2 minutes. Transfer to beef platter to keep warm.
7. Heat 1 tablespoon oil in a wok or saucepan; when it is warm, add garlic, ginger, and chili peppers. Turn heat to high, stir-fry 10 seconds, then add remaining ingredients and stir constantly until sauce boils. Pour the sauce over the beef. Serve immediately.

TO PREPARE AHEAD: Follow steps 1 through 4 in the morning and refrigerate. Before serving, follow steps 5 through 7.

Makes 2–4 servings

KOTA BEEF
KOTA NIU LIU ▪ Hunan

鍋塔牛肉

1 pound sirloin tip or flank steak
2 tablespoons peanut or other salad oil
½ cup peanut or other salad oil
1 clove garlic, chopped
1 cup drained, split, canned baby corn
1 cup frozen peas and carrots
¼ cup drained, canned straw mushrooms

MARINADE:
1 tablespoon cornstarch, dissolved in ¼ cup cold water
2 tablespoons soy sauce
1 tablespoon rice wine or dry sherry
½ teaspoon salt
½ teaspoon sugar
¼ teaspoon baking soda

SEASONING SAUCE:
1 teaspoon cornstarch
3 tablespoons soy sauce
1 tablespoon sugar
1 teaspoon cider vinegar
½ teaspoon salt
½ teaspoon white pepper
¼ cup chicken broth
1 teaspoon hot pepper oil (page 62)

1. Cut the beef with the grain into 2-inch strips; then slice against the grain into thin slices.
2. Mix marinade; add beef and toss to coat. Cover and chill 90 minutes minimum or overnight.
3. Mix 2 tablespoons oil into the marinade to separate pieces of beef.
4. Mix seasoning sauce.
5. Heat ½ cup oil in a wok or a skillet over high heat. Stir-fry beef 1 minute. Remove and drain. Reserve oil.
6. Heat 1 tablespoon reserved oil in the same wok over high heat. Add garlic, baby corn, peas, carrots, and straw mushrooms; stir-fry 1 minute. Add seasoning sauce and stir constantly until sauce thickens. Return the beef to wok and mix well. Serve immediately.

TO PREPARE AHEAD: Follow steps 1–4 and refrigerate. A half-hour ahead, follow step 5. Immediately before serving, follow step 6.

Makes 2–4 servings

SWEET-AND-SOUR WONTONS
TUNG TSU HUN TUN ▪ Canton

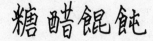

40 wonton wrappers
Peanut or other salad oil for deep-frying

FILLING:
⅓ pound shrimp, shelled, deveined, and washed
⅓ pound ground chuck or pork
¼ cup bamboo shoots, minced
1 tablespoon soy sauce
1 tablespoon rice wine or dry sherry
1 teaspoon salt
½ teaspoon sugar
1 tablespoon cornstarch dissolved in ¼ cup cold water
1 teaspoon sesame-seed oil
2 scallions, minced, including stems
Dash of pepper

SWEET-AND-SOUR SAUCE:
1 tablespoon peanut or other salad oil
1 dried chili pepper, chopped
1 cup 1-inch cubed onion pieces
½ cup cider vinegar
½ cup sugar
1 cup water
2 tablespoons soy sauce
2 tablespoons cornstarch dissolved in ¼ cup cold water
½ cup canned seedless cherries or grapes, drained

1. Mince shrimp and mix well with other filling ingredients in a mixing bowl.

2. Cover wonton wrappers with damp cloth. Place ½ teaspoon filling in one corner of each moistened side. Fold one corner ⅓ over to cover meat. Roll folded corner over once. Wet two unjoined corners and join; press together. Make wontons one at a time, keeping remaining wrappers under cloth so they don't dry out (illustration, page 50).

3. Heat 2 inches of oil in a wok or 3 inches of oil in a deep fryer to 350 degrees. Fry wontons, turning constantly, for 2–3 minutes or until golden brown. Drain and keep hot in 300-degree oven.

4. Heat 1 tablespoon of oil over high heat; stir-fry chili pepper and onion 30 seconds. Add vinegar, sugar, water, and soy sauce; bring to a boil. Stir in dissolved cornstarch and stir constantly until sauce thickens and boils. Add cherries and fried wontons. Mix well. Serve immediately.

TO PREPARE AHEAD: Follow steps 1–3, frying to light brown only, and freeze in a plastic bag. Before serving, bake frozen wontons on a rack in a 375-degree oven 15–20 minutes until crispy and golden brown. Follow step 4 and serve immediately.

Makes 2–4 servings

TEH PAN SIZZLING PLATTER

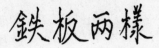

TEH PAN LIANG YANG ▪ Canton

(This dish requires special equipment; see step 8, below.)

½ pound flank steak or fillet
½ pound medium shrimp, shelled, deveined, washed, and patted dry
2 tablespoons peanut or other salad oil
½ cup peanut or other salad oil
1 clove garlic, minced
⅓ cup sliced water chestnuts
½ cup drained, split, canned baby corn
1 cup diagonal-cut, 1-inch celery pieces
¼ pound snow peas
2 scallions, smashed and cut in 1-inch pieces, including stems
½ teaspoon salt

MARINADE:
1 tablespoon cornstarch
1 tablespoon rice wine or dry sherry
1 tablespoon soy sauce
½ teaspoon salt
¼ teaspoon baking soda

SAUCE:
⅓ cup sugar
⅓ cup soy sauce
1 tablespoon cider vinegar
¼ cup chicken broth
1 teaspoon hot-pepper oil (page 62)
¼ teaspoon white pepper
2 teaspoons cornstarch

1. Cut flank steak with the grain in 2-inch strips; slice against the grain ¼-inch thick.

2. Butterfly the shrimp (illustration, page 55).

3. Mix marinade; add beef and shrimp, tossing to coat. Cover and chill one hour.

4. Mix 2 tablespoons oil into the marinade to separate pieces of meat and shrimp.

5. Mix sauce ingredients in a sauce pan. Mix well. Cook over medium heat, stirring constantly, until sauce thickens and boils. Remove to a bowl and keep warm.

6. Heat ½ cup of oil in a wok or skillet until very hot. Stir-fry meat and shrimp 1 minute; remove, drain well and keep warm. Reserve oil.

7. Heat 1 tablespoon reserved oil in a wok or skillet over high heat. Add garlic, water chestnuts, corn, and celery; stir-fry 1 minute. Add snow peas, scallions, and salt; stir-fry 30 seconds. Remove and keep warm.

8. Heat a large aluminum platter until very hot; remove to table and set on a dish liner or protective trivets. Quickly place vegetables and meat on the platter. Pour sauce over, creating sizzling sound effects. Toss quickly with two spoons and serve immediately.

TO PREPARE AHEAD: Follow steps 1–3 and refrigerate. Immediately before serving, follow steps 4–8.

Makes 2–4 servings

TANGERINE-PEEL BEEF
SIANG CHIANG NIU JOU ▪ Hunan

湘江牛肉

1 pound flank steak
½ cup peanut or other salad oil
2 tablespoons peanut or other salad oil
2 tablespoons chopped dried or fresh tangerine peel
2 dried chili peppers, chopped
10 scallions, slightly smashed and cut into 1½-inch pieces, including stems

MARINADE:
1½ tablespoons cornstarch dissolved in ⅓ cup cold water
1 tablespoon rice wine or dry sherry
2 tablespoons soy sauce
½ teaspoon baking soda
½ teaspoon salt
½ teaspoon sugar

SEASONING SAUCE:
3 tablespoons soy sauce
½ tablespoon cider vinegar
⅓ cup orange juice
1 tablespoon sugar
1 teaspoon cornstarch
¼ teaspoon salt

1. Cut flank steak with the grain into 2-inch-wide strips; then slice against the grain ¼-inch thick.
2. Mix marinade and add beef, tossing to coat well. Cover and chill 90 minutes or overnight.
3. Add 1 tablespoon of oil to marinade and mix well to separate beef pieces.
4. Mix seasoning sauce.
5. Heat ½ cup of oil in a wok or skillet until very hot. Stir-fry beef 1 minute; remove and drain well.
6. Warm 1 tablespoon oil in a wok or skillet over medium heat and fry tangerine peel until dark brown. Add chili peppers and scallions; stir-fry 30 seconds. Add seasoning sauce, stirring constantly until sauce thickens and boils. Add beef and mix well. Serve hot.

TO PREPARE AHEAD: Follow steps 1–4 and refrigerate. Immediately before serving, follow steps 5 and 6.

Makes 2–4 servings

TRIPLE DELIGHT WITH SHA CHA SAUCE
SHA CHA SAN YANG ▪ Peking

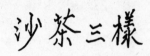

⅓ pound flank steak
¼ pound scallops
1 chicken breast
2 tablespoons peanut or other salad oil
½ cup peanut or other salad oil
1 green pepper, seeded and cut into 1-inch squares
1 cup diagonal-cut, 1-inch celery pieces
½ cup sliced bamboo shoots
1 cup halved mushrooms, fresh or canned
¼ cup roasted cashews

MARINADE:
1 tablespoon cornstarch
1 tablespoon soy sauce
2 tablespoons rice wine or dry sherry
½ teaspoon salt
¼ teaspoon baking soda
Dash of white pepper

SEASONING SAUCE:
1 tablespoon sha cha sauce
1 tablespoon sugar
3 tablespoons soy sauce
½ tablespoon cider vinegar
½ teaspoon salt
1 teaspoon cornstarch
¼ cup chicken broth or water

1. Cut flank steak with grain into 2-inch strips; cut strips into ¼-inch thick slices.

2. Cut scallops horizontally into three slices.

3. Skin and bone chicken breast; cut into 1-inch pieces.

4. Mix marinade; add beef, scallops, and chicken, tossing to coat. Cover and chill 1 hour. Mix in two tablespoons of oil to separate pieces before stir-frying.

5. Mix seasoning sauce.

6. Heat ½ cup of oil in a wok or skillet until very hot. Stir-fry meat mixture 1 minute; remove and drain well. Reserve oil.

7. Heat 1 tablespoon reserved oil in the same wok over high heat. Add green pepper, celery, bamboo shoots, and mushrooms; stir-fry 1 minute. Add seasoning sauce, stirring constantly until sauce thickens and boils. Add meat mixture and mix well. Sprinkle with cashews. Serve hot.

TO PREPARE AHEAD: Follow steps 1–5 and refrigerate. Before serving, follow steps 6 and 7.

Makes 2–4 servings

YU HSIANG BEEF
YU HSIANG RUH SSU ■ Szechuan

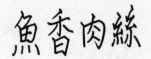

    1 pound sirloin tip or flank steak
    2 tablespoons peanut or other salad oil
    ½ cup peanut or other salad oil
    2 fresh hot peppers, seeded and julienned
    1 fresh, large green pepper, seeded and julienned
    1 carrot, skinned, parboiled 3 minutes, and julienned
    1 cup julienned celery
    1 cup julienned bamboo shoots
    ½ teaspoon salt

MARINADE:
    1 tablespoon cornstarch dissolved in 2 tablespoons cold water
    2 tablespoons soy sauce
    1 tablespoon rice wine or dry sherry
    ½ teaspoon salt
    ½ teaspoon sugar

SEASONING SAUCE:
    1 scallion, minced
    1 teaspoon minced fresh ginger
    1 clove garlic, minced
    2 tablespoons soy sauce
    1 teaspoon cider vinegar
    ¼ cup chicken broth or water
    ½ teaspoon sugar
    ½ teaspoon salt
    1 teaspoon cornstarch
    1 teaspoon sesame-seed oil

1. Slice beef against the grain ⅛-inch thick; cut into 2-inch strips and julienne.

2. Mix marinade and add beef, tossing to coat. Cover and chill 90 minutes.

3. Add 2 tablespoons of oil and mix well to separate pieces of beef.

4. Mix seasoning sauce.

5. Heat ½ cup of oil in a wok or skillet until very hot. Stir-fry beef 30 seconds; remove and drain.

6. Heat reserved tablespoon oil until very hot. Add hot and green peppers, carrot, celery, bamboo shoots, and salt; stir-fry 1 minute. Add seasoning sauce, stirring constantly until it thickens and boils. Add beef, mixing well. Serve hot.

TO PREPARE AHEAD: Follow step 1 and refrigerate. Follow steps 2–4 several hours before serving. To complete, follow steps 5 and 6.

Makes 2–4 servings

ALMOND PORK CHOPS
K'AO P'AI KU ▪ National

杏仁排骨

12 boneless pork chops, about ⅓-inch thick
¼ cup sliced almonds
½ cup fine dried breadcrumbs

MARINADE:
1 clove garlic, minced
1 scallion, chopped, including stems
¼ cup soy sauce
¼ cup rice wine or dry sherry
¼ teaspoon salt
1½ teaspoons sugar
1 tablespoon cornstarch
Dash of pepper

1. Mix marinade and add pork, tossing to coat. Marinate 30 minutes, turning occasionally.
2. On one side only, coat chops with almonds, then breadcrumbs. Coat other side with breadcrumbs only.
3. Bake, almond-side up, in a well-greased pan on the top shelf of the oven, at 325 degrees for 25–30 minutes, or until golden brown. Serve hot.

TO PREPARE AHEAD: Follow steps 1–3, baking 15 minutes only, and refrigerate. Before serving, bake 15–20 minutes longer, or until golden brown.

Makes 6 servings

MOO HSI PORK
MOO HSI RUH ■ Peking

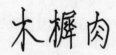

12 mandarin pancakes (page 43)
20 dried golden needles (tiger-lily buds)
2 tablespoons dried Chinese wood ears
4 dried Chinese mushrooms
½ pound lean pork, julienned
6 tablespoons peanut or other salad oil
5 eggs, well beaten
½ cup julienned bamboo shoots
1 teaspoon shredded fresh ginger
2 scallions, julienned, including stems
1 tablespoon soy sauce
1 teaspoon salt

MARINADE:
2 teaspoons cornstarch
1 tablespoon soy sauce
1 tablespoon rice wine or dry sherry
1 teaspoon sesame-seed oil

HOISIN-SAUCE DIP:
¼ cup commercial hoisin sauce
1 tablespoon honey
2 tablespoons soy sauce

1. Make mandarin pancakes.
2. Soak the golden needles in hot water 30 minutes. Wash, drain, stem, and cut in half, crosswise.
3. Soak wood ears in warm water 15 minutes, or until soft. Clean, removing gritty particles, rinse in cold water, drain, and cut into ½-inch pieces.
4. Soak mushrooms in hot water 15 minutes. Drain, stem, and slice paper-thin.
5. Mix marinade and add pork, tossing to coat well. Cover and chill 30 minutes.
6. Heat 4 tablespoons of oil in a wok or skillet until very hot. Add eggs and scramble about 30 seconds. Remove and cut into 1-inch pieces.
7. Heat remaining 2 tablespoons of oil over high heat. Stir-fry pork 2 minutes. Add golden needles, wood ears, mushrooms, bamboo shoots, ginger, scallions, soy sauce, and salt; stir-fry 1 minute. Return the scrambled eggs and mix well. Serve hot with mandarin pancakes and hoisin-sauce dip.
8. To serve: Brush mandarin pancake with 1 teaspoon hoisin-sauce dip. Place 2 tablespoons Moo Hsi Pork on pancake and fold one end (illustration, page 44). Roll into cylinder and eat with fingers.

TO PREPARE AHEAD: Follow steps 1–5 and refrigerate. Two hours before serving, follow steps 6 and 7, but do not mix in egg pieces. Before serving, reheat mixture and add egg pieces. Serve hot.

Makes 2–4 servings

PORK WITH HOT PEPPER
LA TZU RUH TING ■ Szechuan

辣子肉丁

1 pound pork loin or lean pork
2 tablespoons peanut or other salad oil
¼ cup peanut or other salad oil
5 fresh hot peppers, seeded and cut into 1-inch squares
1 green pepper, seeded and cut into 1-inch squares
2 scallions, smashed and cut into 1-inch pieces, including stems
2 cloves garlic, minced
½ cup roasted or fried cashews (page 42)

MARINADE:
2 teaspoons cornstarch
2 tablespoons rice wine or dry sherry
1 tablespoon soy sauce
½ teaspoon salt
Dash of white pepper

SEASONING SAUCE:
1 tablespoon sugar
3 tablespoons soy sauce
½ tablespoon cider vinegar
1 tablespoon rice wine or dry sherry
½ teaspoon salt
1 teaspoon cornstarch

1. Cut the pork with the grain into 1-inch strips; slice strips against the grain ¼-inch thick.
2. Mix marinade and add pork, tossing to coat. Cover and chill 1 hour.
3. Mix seasoning sauce.
4. Add 2 tablespoons of peanut oil to marinade and mix well in order to separate pieces of pork.
5. Heat ¼ cup of oil in a wok or skillet over high heat. Stir-fry pork 2 minutes. Remove and drain well. Reserve the oil.
6. Heat 1 tablespoon reserved oil over high heat. Add hot and green peppers, scallions and garlic; stir-fry 1 minute. Add pork and mix in seasoning sauce, stirring constantly, until sauce thickens and boils. Mix in cashews. Serve hot.

TO PREPARE AHEAD: Follow steps 1 and 2 and refrigerate. A half-hour before serving, follow steps 3–6.

Makes 2–4 servings

SPARERIBS WITH SALTED
BLACK BEANS
TOU SHIH P'AI KU ■ Canton

豆豉排骨

1½ pounds pork spareribs
1 tablespoon peanut or other salad oil
1 clove garlic, crushed
1 tablespoon washed and crushed salted black beans
1 teaspoon shredded fresh ginger
3 tablespoons soy sauce
1 tablespoon sugar
¼ teaspoon salt
1 scallion, chopped, including stems
2 cups water

1. Have your butcher cut the ribs into 1½-inch strips across the bones and separate the ribs. Remove excess fat.

2. Heat oil in a wok or skillet until hot. Stir-fry garlic and black beans 10 seconds. Add spareribs and stir-fry 3 minutes until light brown on both sides. Add ginger, soy sauce, sugar, salt, scallions, and water. Bring to a boil, cover, and cook over medium high heat about 40 minutes, or until ribs become tender. Stir occasionally. If too much liquid evaporates, add boiling water to prevent burning. Serve hot. There should be ½ cup liquid remaining.

NOTE: This dish may be served as a main dish or an appetizer. The quantity of ribs may be doubled, but the seasonings and water must be increased by no more than 50 percent—i.e., one and one-half times the original amounts.

TO PREPARE AHEAD: Follow steps 1 and 2; cover and refrigerate. Before serving, reheat to boiling point and serve hot.

Makes 2–4 servings

STIR-FRIED PORK WITH BEAN THREADS
CHU RUH FEN SSU ■ Peking

猪 肉 粉 絲

½ pound lean pork or beef, julienned
2 ounces dried bean threads
4 tablespoons peanut or other salad oil
2 cups sliced Chinese cabbage
½ pound fresh bean sprouts
½ cup julienned scallions or leeks
2 tablespoons soy sauce
½ teaspoon salt
2 tablespoons chicken broth or water

MARINADE FOR PORK:
1 teaspoon cornstarch
1 tablespoon soy sauce
1 tablespoon rice wine or dry sherry
1 teaspoon sesame-seed oil

1. Mix marinade and add pork, tossing to coat well. Cover and chill 30 minutes.
2. Soak bean threads in warm water 2 minutes, until soft. Drain and cut into 3-inch lengths. Rinse fresh bean sprouts in cold water and drain well.
3. Heat 2 tablespoons of oil in a wok or skillet over high heat. Stir-fry pork 2 minutes. (If using beef, stir-fry 1 minute.) Remove and drain well.
4. Heat 2 tablespoons of oil in a wok or skillet over high heat. Add cabbage, scallions, soy sauce, and salt; stir-fry 1 minute. Add bean threads, bean sprouts, and chicken broth; stir-fry just until bean threads absorb the juices—do not overcook. (If the bean threads become too sticky, add 2 tablespoons or more broth.) Return meat and mix in well. Serve immediately.

NOTE: Bean threads have no flavor themselves, but absorb the other flavors readily. They are easily overcooked and must be served immediately after cooking.

TO PREPARE AHEAD: Follow steps 1 and 2 and refrigerate. Follow steps 3 and 4 immediately before serving.

Makes 4 servings

STIR-FRIED PORK WITH SNOW PEAS
SUEH TOU CHU RUH ▪ Canton

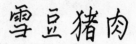

½ pound pork tenderloin or boneless lean pork
1 tablespoon peanut or other salad oil
1 pound fresh snow peas
1 scallion, chopped
½ cup sliced bamboo shoots
1 teaspoon soy sauce
1 tablespoon rice wine or dry sherry
¼ teaspoon salt

MARINADE:
2 teaspoons cornstarch
1 tablespoon soy sauce
2 tablespoons rice wine or dry sherry
½ teaspoon salt
1 teaspoon sesame-seed oil

1. Slice the pork ⅛" thick and cut slices into pieces 1 × 2 inches.
2. Mix marinade and add pork, tossing to coat well. Cover and chill 30 minutes.
3. Heat 1 tablespoon oil in a wok or skillet until very hot. Stir-fry pork 2 minutes. Add snow peas, scallion, bamboo shoots, soy sauce, rice wine, and salt; stir-fry 2 minutes longer. Serve hot.

NOTE: Veal may be used instead of pork.

TO PREPARE AHEAD: Follow steps 1–3 2 hours before serving, omitting snow peas. Before serving, add snow peas and stir-fry 1 minute.

Makes 2 servings

SWEET-AND-SOUR PORK
KU LAO RUH ▪ Canton

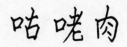

1 pound boneless lean pork
Peanut or other salad oil for deep-frying

MARINADE:
  1 teaspoon chopped fresh ginger
  1 tablespoon soy sauce
  1 tablespoon rice wine or dry sherry

BATTER:
  1 teaspoon salt
  1 egg
  ⅓ cup water
  ½ cup flour
  ⅓ cup cornstarch
  ½ teaspoon baking powder

SWEET-AND-SOUR SAUCE:
  1 tablespoon peanut or other salad oil
  1 clove garlic, minced
  1 cup 1-inch cubed onion pieces
  2 tablespoons soy sauce
  1 tablespoon tomato paste
  ⅓ cup cider vinegar
  ⅓ cup packed brown sugar
  ⅔ cup cold water
  ⅓ cup canned-pineapple syrup
  1½ tablespoons cornstarch dissolved in ¼ cup cold water
  ½ cup drained pineapple chunks
  1 green pepper, seeded and cut into 1-inch pieces
  1 tomato, peeled, seeded, and cut into 1-inch wedges

1. Slice the pork ⅓-inch thick; cut slices into 1 × 1-inch pieces.
2. Mix marinade and add pork, tossing to coat well. Cover and chill 15 minutes.
3. Combine batter ingredients; mix until free of lumps.
4. Heat 1 inch of oil in a wok or skillet over high heat. Dip pork in batter and fry, a few pieces at a time, until golden brown. Drain and keep warm in oven.
5. Heat 1 tablespoon of oil in a saucepan or wok over high heat. Stir-fry garlic and onion until onion is transparent. Blend in soy sauce, tomato paste, vinegar, brown sugar, water, and pineapple syrup; bring the mixture to a boil. Stir in dissolved cornstarch and stir constantly until sauce thickens and boils. Mix in pineapple, green pepper, and tomato wedges. Pour sauce over pork. Serve immediately.

NOTE: Veal may be used in place of pork.

TO PREPARE AHEAD: Follow steps 1 and 2; cover and refrigerate. Several hours before serving, cut pineapple, green pepper, and tomato wedges; refrigerate in plastic bags. Then follow steps 3 through 5, omitting dissolved cornstarch, pineapple, and vegetables. To complete, reheat pork 5–8 minutes in a preheated 400-degree oven. Bring sauce to a boil again; mix in dissolved cornstarch, pineapple, and vegetables.

Makes 2–4 servings

SWEET-AND-SOUR SPARERIBS
T'IEN SUAN P'AI KU ▪ Shanghai

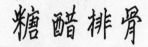

2 pounds trimmed pork spareribs (about 2½ pounds before trimming)
8 cups water
2 teaspoons salt
¼ teaspoon five-spice powder (optional)
2 tablespoons soy sauce
2 tablespoons rice wine or dry sherry
1 egg
½ cup cornstarch
Peanut or other salad oil for deep-frying

SWEET-AND-SOUR SAUCE:
1 tablespoon peanut or other salad oil
1 clove garlic, minced
1 medium carrot, peeled and cut diagonally into 1-inch chunks
⅓ cup cider vinegar
⅓ cup sugar
2 tablespoons soy sauce
½ cup water
½ cup pineapple juice
1½ tablespoons cornstarch dissolved in 3 tablespoons cold water
½ cup drained pineapple chunks
¼ cup drained canned seedless grapes

1. Have your butcher cut the ribs into 2-inch strips across the bones.
2. Heat 8 cups water in a saucepan; add ribs and 2 teaspoons salt. Bring to a boil, then reduce heat to medium and cook, covered, 15 minutes. Drain, cool, and cut into individual rib pieces.
3. Mix five-spice powder, soy sauce, rice wine, and egg; add ribs and toss to coat. Sprinkle cornstarch over ribs; toss again. Set aside.
4. Heat 2 inches of oil to 375 degrees in a wok or a deep-fryer. Fry ribs for 3–5 minutes or until golden brown. Drain.
5. Heat 1 tablespoon of oil in a wok or saucepan over medium heat. Stir-fry garlic 10 seconds. Add carrot and stir-fry 1 minute. Blend in vinegar, sugar, soy sauce, water, and pineapple juice; bring to a boil. Stir in dissolved cornstarch, stirring constantly until sauce thickens and boils. Add pineapple, grapes, and ribs; mix well. Serve immediately.

TO PREPARE AHEAD: Follow steps 1–3; cover and refrigerate. A few hours before serving, fry ribs and prepare sauce ingredients. Before serving, re-fry ribs until crispy or reheat 10–15 minutes in a 375-degree oven. Then follow step 5 to make sauce.

Makes 4 servings

POULTRY

鷄　鴨

BON BON CHICKEN
BON BON GEE ■ Szechuan

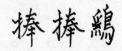

棒棒鷄

1 chicken, broiler or fryer, 3½ pounds
3 quarts water
1 scallion, including stems
3 thin slices fresh ginger
1 large cucumber
1 teaspoon salt

SEASONING SAUCE:
1 tablespoon sesame-seed paste (page 41) or 2 tablespoons peanut butter
1 tablespoon hot-pepper oil (page 62)
1 tablespoon sesame-seed oil
3 tablespoons soy sauce
2 tablespoons cider vinegar
2½ teaspoons sugar
½ teaspoon salt
1 teaspoon Szechuan peppercorn powder (page 41)
1 teaspoon minced fresh ginger
1 tablespoon minced parsley
2 cloves garlic, minced

1. Prepare sesame-seed paste, hot-pepper oil, and Szechuan peppercorn powder.
2. Clean the chicken and dry with paper towels. In a large saucepan, bring the water to a boil. Add chicken, scallion, and ginger. Cover and cook for about 15 minutes on each side over medium heat. Pierce the thigh of the chicken with a fork; if no blood escapes, chicken is done. Allow to cool. Reserve broth for soup.
3. Peel cucumber, split lengthwise and remove seeds. Slice crosswise ⅛-inch thick. Add 1 teaspoon salt and mix well. Let stand for 10 minutes, then squeeze out the juice and reserve.
4. Skin and bone chicken. With fingers, shred the chicken into 2-inch shreds. Place on serving platter, arranging cucumber around chicken. Chill if desired.
5. Mix sesame-seed paste, hot-pepper oil, and sesame-seed oil. Add soy sauce 1 tablespoon at a time; mix well each time. Add vinegar, sugar, Szechuan peppercorn powder, ginger, parsley; and garlic; mix well. Chill if desired.

6. Pour sauce over chicken and mix well. Serve chilled or at room temperature.

TO PREPARE AHEAD: Follow steps 1–5; cover and refrigerate. Before serving, follow step 6.

Makes 4 servings

CHICKEN WITH CASHEWS
YUO KOO GEE TING ▪ Peking

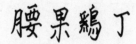

2 pounds chicken breasts
2 tablespoons peanut or other salad oil
¼ cup peanut or other salad oil
1 clove garlic, minced
2 scallions, chopped, including stems
1 green pepper, seeds removed, cut into ½-inch cubes
½ cup sliced bamboo shoots
½ cup sliced water chestnuts
2 teaspoons cornstarch dissolved in 2 tablespoons cold water
¼ cup toasted cashews or toasted walnuts

MARINADE:
1 tablespoon cornstarch
1 tablespoon soy sauce
1 tablespoon rice wine or dry sherry
¾ teaspoon salt
Dash of white pepper

SEASONING SAUCE:
3 tablespoons soy sauce
1 tablespoon rice wine or dry sherry
½ teaspoon sugar
½ cup chicken broth
Dash of white pepper

1. Skin and bone the chicken; cut into ½-inch cubes.
2. Mix marinade and add chicken, tossing to coat. Cover and chill 30 minutes.
3. Add 1 tablespoon or more oil to marinade and mix well to separate chicken pieces.
4. Mix seasoning sauce.
5. Heat ¼ cup of oil in a wok or skillet until very hot. Stir-fry chicken 1 minute. Remove and drain well.
6. Heat remaining tablespoon of oil until very hot. Add garlic, scallion, green pepper, bamboo shoots, and water chestnuts; stir-fry 1 minute. Blend in the seasoning sauce and bring to a boil, uncovered. Stir in dissolved cornstarch and stir constantly until sauce thickens and boils. Add chicken and mix well. Serve hot, with cashews sprinkled on top.

TO PREPARE AHEAD: Follow steps 1 and 2; cover and refrigerate. Before serving, follow steps 3–6.

Makes 2–4 servings

CHAMPAGNE CHICKEN
HSIANG PIN GEE ■ Canton

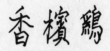

   2 whole chicken breasts
   4 tablespoons peanut or other salad oil
   1 cup peanut or other salad oil
   1 large carrot
   2 scallions, julienned, including stems

MARINADE:
   1 tablespoon cornstarch
   1 teaspoon salt
   1 tablespoon rice wine or dry sherry
   1 large egg white
   Dash white pepper

CHAMPAGNE SAUCE:
   1 teaspoon minced fresh ginger
   1 teaspoon salt
   1 tablespoon sugar
   ½ cup champagne
   ½ cup chicken broth
   ¼ teaspoon white pepper
   2 teaspoons cornstarch

1. Skin and bone the chicken; slice paper-thin against the grain.
2. Mix marinade and add chicken, tossing to coat. Cover and chill 1 hour.
3. Peel carrot and boil 2 minutes. Cool in cold water and julienne.
4. Add 3 tablespoons of oil to marinade; mix well to separate pieces of chicken.
5. Mix champagne sauce.
6. Heat 1 cup of oil in a wok or skillet until just hot. Stir-fry chicken 1 minute. Remove and drain, reserving oil.
7. Heat 1 tablespoon of oil in a wok over high heat. Stir-fry carrot and scallions 20 seconds. Add champagne sauce, stirring constantly until sauce thickens. Add chicken and mix well. Serve hot.

TO PREPARE AHEAD: Follow steps 1–3; refrigerate. Before serving, follow steps 4–7.

Makes 2–4 servings

FRIED SESAME CHICKEN
CHA TZU GEE ▪ Peking

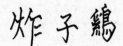

1 chicken, broiler or fryer, 3 to 3½ pounds
1 tablespoon Szechuan peppercorn salt if not using brown sauce (page 41)
Peanut or other salad oil for deep-frying

MARINADE:
1 scallion, minced, including stems
2 thin slices fresh ginger, minced
¼ cup soy sauce
2 tablespoons rice wine or dry sherry
1 teaspoon salt
1 teaspoon sugar
1 egg
½ cup cornstarch
2 tablespoons sesame seeds

BROWN SAUCE (optional):
1 tablespoon peanut or other salad oil
1 clove garlic, minced
1 scallion, chopped, including stems
½ tablespoon cider vinegar
½ cup chicken broth
1 tablespoon soy sauce
¼ teaspoon salt
2 teaspoons sugar
1½ teaspoons cornstarch dissolved in 2 tablespoons cold water

1. Clean the chicken and dry; cut (with skin and bones, to be authentic) into 1 × 2-inch pieces.
2. Mix marinade and add chicken, tossing to coat. Cover and chill 1 hour.
3. Heat 2–3 inches of oil to 375 degrees in a wok or deep-fryer. Fry chicken 3 minutes until light brown. Drain. Re-fry chicken 1 minute until golden brown. Serve hot with peppercorn salt, or set aside and continue to next step.
4. Heat 1 tablespoon of oil in a wok or skillet until very hot. Stir-fry garlic and scallion 10 seconds. Add vinegar, chicken broth, soy sauce, salt, and sugar; bring to a boil. Add dissolved cornstarch and stir constantly until sauce thickens and boils. Add chicken and mix well. Serve immediately.

TO PREPARE AHEAD: Follow steps 1–3, frying chicken once only. Before serving, re-fry until golden brown. Serve with peppercorn salt or brown sauce (step 4).

Makes 2–4 servings

LYCHEE CHICKEN
LI CHIH CHI ▪ Canton

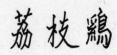

2 whole chicken breasts
½ cup cornstarch
Peanut or other salad oil for deep-frying

MARINADE:
½ teaspoon salt
1 teaspoon soy sauce
1 egg
1 tablespoon sesame seeds

SAUCE:
1 tablespoon peanut or other salad oil
1 clove garlic, minced
¼ cup cider vinegar
¼ cup sugar
¼ cup lychee syrup (reserved from lychees)
¼ cup water
1 tablespoon cornstarch dissolved in ¼ cup cold water
⅔ cup canned, drained lychees
¼ cup drained pineapple chunks
¼ cup pitted dark cherries
1 tablespoon slivered toasted almonds

1. Skin and bone the chicken breasts; cut into 1-inch cubes.
2. Mix marinade and add chicken, tossing to coat. Marinate chicken for 5 minutes.
3. Coat chicken heavily with cornstarch. Arrange chicken on a floured cookie sheet (do not stack).
4. Heat 1 inch of oil in a wok or skillet until very hot. Fry chicken until light brown. Drain and keep warm in oven.
5. Heat 1 tablespoon of oil over high heat. Lightly brown garlic. Blend in vinegar, sugar, lychee syrup, and water; bring to a boil. Stir in dissolved cornstarch; stir constantly until sauce thickens and boils. Add lychees, pineapple chunks, and cherries. Pour sauce over chicken and sprinkle with sliced almonds. Serve at once.

TO PREPARE AHEAD: Follow steps 1–4, frying chicken only very light brown. Follow step 5 to make the sauce, but omit fruits and cornstarch. Before serving, re-fry chicken to light brown or reheat 10–15 minutes in a 375-degree oven. Bring sauce to a boil, stir in dissolved cornstarch and fruits, stirring until sauce thickens and boils. Pour sauce over chicken, sprinkle with almonds, and serve at once.

Makes 2–4 servings

ORANGE SESAME CHICKEN
CHU TZU GEE ■ Peking

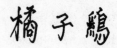

2 whole chicken breasts
Flour for dusting
1 ounce rice sticks
Peanut or other salad oil for deep-frying
1 tablespoon toasted sesame seeds

MARINADE:
1 tablespoon rice wine or dry sherry
½ teaspoon salt
Dash of white pepper

BATTER:
½ cup cold water
½ teaspoon salt
⅓ cup cornstarch
⅓ cup all-purpose flour
⅓ cup sesame seeds
½ teaspoon baking powder
1 teaspoon soy sauce

ORANGE SAUCE:
1¼ cups fresh orange juice
1 tablespoon cider vinegar
3 tablespoons sugar
1 tablespoon orange liqueur or orange extract
1 tablespoon cornstarch

1. Skin and bone and butterfly-cut (illustration, page 55) the chicken breasts.
2. Mix marinade and add chicken, tossing to coat well. Cover and chill 10 minutes.
3. Toss chicken with flour in a plastic bag; coat well.
4. Combine batter ingredients; mix until smooth and free of lumps.
5. Heat 1" of oil in a wok or deep-fryer to 400 degrees. Test with one piece of rice stick: Within 3 seconds the rice stick added to oil should puff. When oil is ready, fry rice sticks 3 seconds. Turn and fry the other side 3 seconds. Drain and cool. Break into 1-inch pieces and sprinkle on serving platter.
6. Heat ½-inch of oil in a wok or skillet to 375 degrees. Dip chicken in batter and fry both sides until golden brown. Drain.
7. Cut fried breasts into 1-inch sections and place on platter atop rice sticks. Keep warm.
8. Mix orange-sauce ingredients and cook over medium heat, stirring until sauce thickens and boils. Pour sauce over chicken and sprinkle with toasted sesame seeds. Serve immediately.

TO PREPARE AHEAD: Follow steps 1–6, frying chicken light brown only. Refrigerate in a plastic bag. Store rice sticks in a plastic bag at room temperature. Before serving, re-fry chicken until golden brown and follow steps 7 and 8.

Makes 2–4 servings

PALACE CHICKEN
KUNG PAO GEE TING ▪ Szechuan

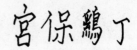

2 whole chicken breasts or whole broiler-fryer
2 tablespoons peanut or other salad oil
½ cup peanut or other salad oil
3 dried chili peppers, halved
1 teaspoon minced fresh ginger
2 scallions, cut into 1-inch sections, including stems
½ cup sliced bamboo shoots
½ cup skinned, fried peanuts (page 42)

MARINADE:
1 tablespoon cornstarch
2 tablespoons soy sauce

SEASONING SAUCE:
2 tablespoons soy sauce
1 tablespoon rice wine or dry sherry
½ tablespoon cider vinegar
1 tablespoon water
2 teaspoons sugar
½ teaspoon salt
1 teaspoon cornstarch
1 teaspoon sesame-seed oil

1. Skin and bone the chicken; then cut into ½-inch cubes.
2. Mix marinade and add chicken, tossing to coat. Cover and chill 30 minutes.
3. Add 2 tablespoons of oil to marinade; mix well to separate pieces of chicken.
4. Mix seasoning sauce and set aside.
5. Heat ½ cup of oil in a wok or skillet until very hot. Stir-fry chicken 1 minute. Remove and drain well. Reserve oil.
6. Heat 1 tablespoon reserved oil until hot. Add chili peppers, ginger, scallions, and bamboo shoots; stir-fry 1 minute. Add seasoning sauce and stir constantly until it thickens and boils.
7. Return chicken and stir-fry 30 seconds. Mix in peanuts. Serve immediately.

TO PREPARE AHEAD: Follow steps 1 and 2; cover and refrigerate. Follow steps 3–6 several hours before cooking. Before serving, follow step 7.

Makes 2–4 servings

PRESSED BEANCAKE WITH CHICKEN
TOU FU KA GEE TING ▪ Peking

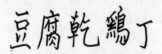

    2 whole chicken breasts or 4 legs
    2 tablespoons peanut or other salad oil
    ½ cup peanut or other salad oil
    1 clove garlic, minced
    1 dried chili pepper, chopped
    2 scallions, smashed and cut into 1-inch pieces, including stems
    2 squares pressed beancake, cut into ½-inch cubes
    ½ cup well-drained canned straw mushrooms
    ½ cup ½-inch cubed bamboo shoots
    ½ cup peanuts, toasted or fried (page 42)

MARINADE:
    ½ teaspoon salt
    1 tablespoon cornstarch
    1 tablespoon soy sauce
    1 tablespoon rice wine or dry sherry

SEASONING SAUCE:
    1 tablespoon sugar
    2 tablespoons soy sauce
    1 tablespoon commercial hoisin sauce
    ½ teaspoon salt
    1 teaspoon cider vinegar
    1 teaspoon cornstarch
    2 tablespoons chicken broth or water
    Dash of black pepper

1. Skin and bone chicken; cut into ½-inch cubes.
2. Mix marinade and add chicken, tossing to coat. Cover and chill 1 hour.
3. Add 2 tablespoons of oil to marinade; mix well to separate chicken pieces.
4. Mix seasoning sauce.
5. Heat ½ cup of oil in a wok or skillet until very hot. Stir-fry chicken 1 minute. Remove and drain; reserve oil.
6. Heat 1 tablespoon reserved oil in a wok or skillet over high heat. Add garlic, chili, and scallions; stir-fry 10 seconds. Add beancake, mushrooms, and bamboo shoots; stir-fry 1 minute. Add seasoning sauce, stirring constantly until it thickens and boils.
7. Return chicken; mix well. Remove to a serving platter and sprinkle peanuts on top. Serve hot.

TO PREPARE AHEAD: Follow steps 1–4; refrigerate. Before serving, follow steps 5–7.

Makes 2–4 servings

STIR-FRIED CHICKEN WITH RICE STICKS
MA I SHANG SU ▪ Szechuan

螞蟻上樹

1 whole chicken breast or 2 legs
2 tablespoons peanut or other salad oil
Peanut or other salad oil for deep-frying
¼ pound rice sticks

MARINADE:
¼ teaspoon salt
2 teaspoons soy sauce
1 tablespoon rice wine or dry sherry
1 teaspoon cornstarch

SAUCE:
1 tablespoon peanut or other salad oil
4 dried Chinese mushrooms, stemmed, soaked in hot water 15 minutes, and chopped
½ cup diced bamboo shoots
½ cup diced water chestnuts
½ cup diced celery
½ cup diced carrots, parboiled
1 teaspoon salt
½ teaspoon sugar
1 tablespoon soy sauce
1⅓ cups chicken broth
1½ tablespoons cornstarch dissolved in 3 tablespoons cold water

1. Skin, bone, and dice the chicken.
2. Mix marinade and add chicken, tossing to coat. Marinate 10 minutes.
3. Heat 2 tablespoons of oil in a wok or skillet over high heat. Stir-fry chicken 1 minute. Drain.
4. Heat 1 tablespoon of oil over high heat. Add mushrooms, bamboo shoots, water chestnuts, celery, and carrots; stir-fry 1 minute. Blend in salt, sugar, soy sauce, and chicken broth; bring to a boil. Add dissolved cornstarch and stir constantly until sauce thickens and boils. Return chicken and mix well. Remove and set aside.
5. Heat 3 inches oil to 425 degrees in a wok or deep-fryer. Fry rice sticks only 3 seconds on each side. Do not overcook; rice sticks should puff up almost immediately. Drain and place on serving platter at the table. Immediately pour chicken and sauce over rice sticks producing festive sizzling sounds.

NOTE: Use one piece of rice stick to test the oil. If the oil is hot enough the rice stick will puff up in 3 seconds. It is very important to fry rice sticks in very hot oil immediately before serving.

TO PREPARE AHEAD: Follow step 1; refrigerate. Follow steps 2–4 hours ahead. Immediately before serving, reheat sauce and follow step 5.

Makes 4 servings

STUFFED WALNUT CHICKEN
SIANG GEE HSIUNG ▪ Peking

½ cup ginger sauce (page 64)
2 whole chicken breasts
1 teaspoon salt
Dash of white pepper
1 tablespoon rice wine or dry sherry
Flour for coating
¼ cup chopped walnuts
Peanut or other salad oil for deep-frying

FILLING:
⅓ pound ground chuck
¼ pound small shrimp, shelled, deveined and washed
¼ cup minced water chestnuts
1 scallion, minced, including stems
¾ teaspoon salt
1 teaspoon sesame-seed oil
1 tablespoon rice wine or dry sherry
2 teaspoons cornstarch dissolved in 1 tablespoon cold water
1 egg white

BATTER:
½ cup cornstarch dissolved in 1 cup cold water
⅔ cup all-purpose flour
⅓ cup sweet rice flour
1 teaspoon salt
1 teaspoon baking powder
1 egg yolk

1. Prepare ginger sauce.
2. Skin and bone the chicken breasts. Split in half lengthwise.
3. Mix with salt, pepper, and rice wine; let stand 10 minutes.
4. Dust chicken with flour.
5. Mix filling well and spread on chicken. Then sprinkle walnuts on filling and pat down.
6. Combine batter ingredients; mix until smooth and free of lumps.
7. Heat ½-inch of oil in skillet over high heat. Dip chicken into batter and fry stuffed-side down 2–3 minutes; turn and fry 1 minute or until both sides are golden brown. Drain.
8. Cut chicken into 1-inch pieces. Serve hot with ginger sauce.

TO PREPARE AHEAD: Follow steps 1–7, frying light brown only, a few days before, and freeze in plastic bag. Refrigerate. Before serving, re-fry thawed chicken or bake on a rack 10–15 minutes in a preheated 375-degree oven until golden brown and crisp. Then follow step 8.

Makes 4 servings

THREE-KINGDOM CHICKEN
CHAO SAN TING ▪ Canton

炒三丁

    ¼ pound sirloin tip or flank steak
    1 whole chicken breast
    ¼ pound medium shrimp, shelled, deveined and washed
    5 tablespoons peanut or other salad oil
    1 clove garlic, chopped
    1 teaspoon chopped fresh ginger
    1 scallion, chopped, including stems
    ½ cup sliced bamboo shoots
    ½ cup sliced water chestnuts
    ½ cup diagonally-sliced 1-inch celery pieces
    1 cup halved mushrooms
    ¼ cup blanched whole almonds, fried (page 42)

MARINADE:
    2 tablespoons rice wine or dry sherry
    1 teaspoon salt
    1 tablespoon cornstarch

SEASONING SAUCE:
    1 tablespoon soy sauce
    2 tablespoons rice wine or dry sherry
    1 teaspoon salt
    ½ teaspoon sugar
    Dash of pepper
    ½ cup chicken broth
    1 tablespoon cornstarch dissolved in 2 tablespoons cold water

1. Slice the beef ⅛-inch thick; cut slices into 1-inch squares.
2. Skin and bone the chicken breast; cut into ⅔ inch cubes.
3. Butterfly-cut the shrimp (illustration, page 55).
4. Mix marinade and add meat, chicken, and shrimp, tossing to coat. Cover and chill for 10 minutes.
5. Mix seasoning sauce.
6. Heat 4 tablespoons of oil in a wok or skillet over high heat. Stir-fry meat, chicken, and shrimp 2 minutes. Remove and set aside.
7. Heat remaining tablespoon of oil until very hot. Add garlic, ginger, scallion, bamboo shoots, water chestnuts, celery, and mushrooms; stir-fry 1 minute. Add seasoning sauce, stir constantly until it thickens and boils. Return meat, chicken, and shrimp; mix well. Garnish with deep-fried almonds. Serve hot.

NOTE: Other combinations of meat, poultry, and seafood may be used.

TO PREPARE AHEAD: Follow steps 1–4; refrigerate. Before serving, follow steps 5–7.

Makes 2–4 servings

PEKING DUCK
PEI CHING K'OA YA ▪ Peking

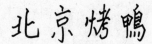

1 dozen Mandarin pancakes (page 43)
1 dozen scallion brushes (page 45)
1 duckling, 4–5 pounds
2 tablespoons salt
2 cups rice wine or dry sherry
Soy sauce for coating

DIPPING SAUCE:
2 tablespoons commercial hoisin sauce
2 teaspoons soy sauce
1 teaspoon honey

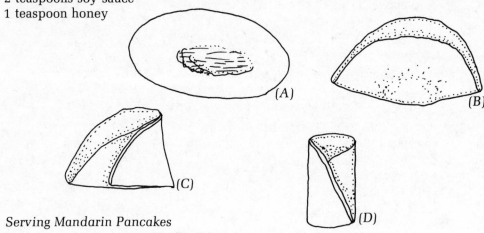

Serving Mandarin Pancakes

1. Prepare Mandarin pancakes and scallion brushes.
2. Wash the duck, removing glands near neck and shoulder, and excess fat from cavity. Pat dry; rub with 2 tablespoons salt inside and out.
3. Place duck in a 3-quart oval casserole with 2 cups rice wine. Cover and chill 3–6 hours, turning once. Drain ducks.
4. Place duck on a 10-inch pie plate and steam 45–50 minutes.
5. Drain duck and pat dry; rub with soy sauce to give skin golden color.
6. Roast breast-side up, wings wrapped in foil to prevent charring, in a preheated 300-degree oven 90 minutes–2 hours or until skin is lightly brown and crispy. Transfer to heated platter.
7. Mix dipping sauce.
8. Cut duck meat (with skin) into 2 × 2-inch pieces. Using a scallion brush, brush ½ teaspoon dipping sauce on Mandarin pancake. Put a piece of duck on each pancake (a); fold in half (b). Fold ⅓ of one end over (c), then roll (open end first) (d) and eat.

NOTE: Reserve rice wine for use in other dishes.

TO PREPARE AHEAD: Follow step 1; refrigerate (pancakes can be frozen). Follow steps 2–5 the day before; refrigerate. Two hours before serving follow steps 6–8.

Makes 4–6 servings

PRESSED DUCK
KUO SHAO YA ▪ Peking

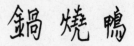

1 duckling, 4–5 pounds
Peanut or other salad oil for deep-frying
2 cutting boards or planks (approximately 12 × 24 inches) for pressing

MARINADE:
1 tablespoon minced fresh ginger root
1 clove garlic, minced
1 teaspoon salt
½ teaspoon black pepper
2 tablespoons soy sauce
1 tablespoon rice wine or dry sherry
1 tablespoon honey

COATING:
⅔ cup fine dried breadcrumbs
¼ cup sliced almonds

EGG WASH:
3 eggs, slightly beaten
1 teaspoon salt
½ teaspoon white pepper

ORANGE SAUCE:
8 ounces orange marmalade
¼ cup sliced carrots
⅓ cup sugar
⅓ cup cider vinegar
½ cup water
¼ cup fruit juice (from fruit listed below)
2½ tablespoons cornstarch dissolved in 3 tablespoons cold water
½ cup drained pineapple chunks (reserve syrup)
½ cup drained, canned pineapple chunks (reserve syrup)
½ cup drained, canned Mandarin oranges (reserve syrup)
1 small tomato, skinned and cut into 1-inch cubes
2 tablespoons sliced almonds

1. Wash the duck, removing glands near neck and shoulder, and excess fat from cavity. Dry inside and out.
2. Mix marinade; rub the duck inside and out. Cover and chill 1 hour.
3. Steam duck in a large bowl 1 hour and 15 minutes.
4. Mix egg wash.
5. Drain duck and remove skin while still hot; then remove meat and cut into 1-inch pieces.
6. Cover a cutting board first with foil, then with plastic wrap, and cover half the surface with duck meat, packing it closely (a).
7. Brush with egg wash; sprinkle with almonds and breadcrumbs.
8. Fold plastic and foil over meat (b) and lightly seal (c); turn over carefully and re-open to add remaining egg wash, almonds, and breadcrumbs to other side of duck.

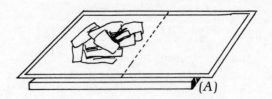

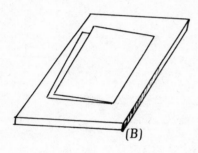

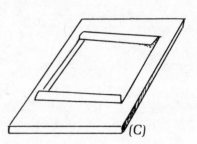

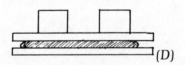

Making Pressed Duck

9. Reseal, place second cutting board on top and weight or clamp well 1 hour to press duck (d); remove to freezer, still between boards (see illustration above). Freeze solid.

10. Heat ½ inch of oil in a skillet over medium heat. Cut frozen duck into quarters and fry one at a time until both sides are golden brown. Drain well on paper towels and cut into 1 × 2-inch pieces. Hold in warm oven.

11. Combine marmalade, carrots, sugar, vinegar, water, and fruit syrup in a medium saucepan; stir in dissolved cornstarch and cook, stirring constantly, until sauce thickens and boils. Immediately before serving add pineapple, oranges, and tomato. Mix thoroughly. Pour over duck and garnish with sliced almonds. Serve immediately.

TO PREPARE AHEAD: Follow steps 1–9 up to 3 weeks ahead; step 10, 1–2 days before. To complete, bake fried duck 10–15 minutes in a preheated 400-degree oven and follow step 11.

Makes 4–6 servings

STIR-FRIED BONELESS DUCK
CHIEN TSENG YA ▪ Canton

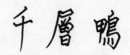

½ duckling, about 2½ pounds
½ tablespoon salt
1 tablespoon rice wine or dry sherry
Cornstarch for coating
Peanut or other salad oil for deep-frying

BATTER:
½ cup water
1 teaspoon salt
¼ teaspoon baking soda
¼ cup cornstarch
¼ cup sweet rice flour
¼ cup all-purpose flour

SEASONINGS:
1 tablespoon soy sauce
1 tablespoon oyster sauce
½ teaspoon salt
Dash of pepper
½ cup chicken broth
1½ teaspoons cornstarch

SAUCE:
1 tablespoon peanut or other salad oil
1 scallion, chopped, including stems
4 dried Chinese black mushrooms, soaked in hot water 15 minutes,
    stemmed and quartered
½ cup sliced water chestnuts
1 cup diagonally sliced celery
½ cup drained, canned straw mushrooms or fresh mushrooms
½ cup broccoli florets

1. Wash the duck, removing glands and fat near neck and shoulder, and excess fat from cavity.
2. Rub the duck inside and out with salt and sherry.
3. Steam on a shallow plate 45 minutes until tender.
4. Remove skin; bone and cut meat into 1-inch cubes.
5. Combine all batter ingredients; mix until free of lumps. Dip duck pieces into batter and coat lightly with cornstarch. Set aside on floured waxed paper; do not stack.
6. Heat 2–3 inches of oil to 375 degrees in a wok or deep-fryer. Fry duck until golden brown. Drain well and hold in a 350-degree oven.
7. Mix seasonings.
8. Heat 1 tablespoon of oil over high heat. Add scallion, mushrooms, water chestnuts, celery, straw mushrooms, and broccoli; stir-fry 2 minutes. Add seasonings and stir constantly until sauce thickens and boils. Return fried duck and mix well. Serve immediately.

TO PREPARE AHEAD: Follow steps 1–6, frying to light brown only; refrigerate. Before serving, re-fry duck to golden brown and follow steps 7 and 8.

Makes 2–4 servings

SEAFOOD

海 鮮

BABY SHRIMP WITH PINE NUTS
SUNG TZU HAIA ■ Szechuan

松子蝦仁

1 pound small shrimp, shelled, deveined, washed, and patted dry
2 tablespoons peanut or other salad oil
½ cup peanut or other salad oil
½ cup ½-inch cubed bamboo shoots
1 green pepper, seeded and ½-inch cubed
½ cup pine nuts, toasted

MARINADE:
1 tablespoon cornstarch dissolved in 1 tablespoon rice wine or dry sherry
½ teaspoon salt
¼ teaspoon baking soda
½ egg white
Dash of white pepper

SEASONINGS:
½ tablespoon hot chili paste
1 tablespoon tomato paste
1 tablespoon soy sauce
2 tablespoons sugar
2 tablespoons rice wine or dry sherry
1 teaspoon cornstarch dissolved in 2 tablespoons cold water
1 clove garlic, minced
1 tablespoon minced fresh ginger
2 scallions, minced, including stems

1. Mix marinade and add shrimp, tossing to coat. Cover and chill 2 hours.
2. Mix seasonings.
3. Add 2 tablespoons oil to marinade; mix well to separate shrimp.
4. Heat ½ cup of oil in a wok or skillet until very hot. Stir-fry shrimp 1 minute until pink. Remove and drain well.
5. Heat 1 tablespoon reserved oil in a wok or skillet over high heat. Add bamboo shoots and green peppers; stir-fry 1 minute. Add seasonings, stirring until sauce thickens and boils. Return the shrimp; mix well. Serve hot, sprinkled with pine nuts.

TO PREPARE AHEAD: Follow steps 1–3; cover and refrigerate. Before serving, follow steps 4 and 5.

Makes 2–4 servings

CURRY SHRIMP
CHIA LI HSIA ▪ Canton

咖 哩 蝦

1 pound medium shrimp, shelled, deveined, washed, and patted dry
3 tablespoons peanut or other salad oil
1 cup peanut or other salad oil
½ tablespoon curry powder
2 teaspoons cold water
2 cups ½-inch cubed onion pieces

MARINADE:
½ teaspoon salt
⅛ teaspoon baking soda
1 tablespoon cornstarch
Dash of white pepper
1 tablespoon rice wine or dry sherry

SEASONING SAUCE:
2 teaspoons soy sauce
¼ teaspoon salt
¼ cup chicken broth
½ teaspoon cornstarch dissolved in 1 tablespoon cold water

1. Butterfly-cut the shrimp (illustration, page 55).
2. Mix marinade and add shrimp, tossing to coat. Cover and chill at least 1 hour or overnight.
3. Mix seasonings.
4. Mix 3 tablespoons of hot oil into marinade to separate shrimp.
5. Heat 1 cup of oil in a wok or skillet until very hot. Stir-fry shrimp 1 minute. Drain and reserve oil.
6. Mix curry and 2 teaspoons water into a smooth paste.
7. Heat 1 tablespoon reserved oil over medium heat. When just warm, add curry paste and stir-fry 15 seconds. Add onions. Raise heat to high and stir-fry onion until transparent (about 90 seconds).
8. Add seasonings, stirring until sauce thickens and boils. Return shrimp and mix well. Serve hot.

TO PREPARE AHEAD: Follow steps 1 and 2 the day before; refrigerate. Before serving, follow steps 3–8.

Makes 2–4 servings

LAKE TUNG TING SEAFOOD
SIANG CHI HAI SIEN ▪ Hunan

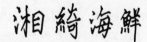

½ pound lobster tail, shelled, washed, and patted dry
⅓ pound medium shrimp, shelled, deveined, washed, and patted dry
⅓ pound scallops
2 tablespoons peanut or other salad oil
½ cup peanut or other salad oil

SEASONINGS:
  2 tablespoons soy sauce
  1 teaspoon salt
  1 teaspoon sugar
  2 teaspoons cornstarch
  1 teaspoon sesame-seed oil
  ½ cup chicken broth

MARINADE FOR SEAFOOD:
  1 tablespoon cornstarch
  2 tablespoons rice wine or dry sherry
  ½ teaspoon salt
  Dash of white pepper

SAUCE:
  1 tablespoon peanut or other salad oil
  2 dried chili peppers, chopped
  1 teaspoon minced fresh ginger
  2 teaspoons washed and crushed salted black beans
  1 scallion, chopped, including stems
  ½ cup ½ × 1-inch cooked ham squares
  10 small dried Chinese black mushrooms, soaked in hot water 15 minutes
     and stemmed
  ⅔ cup sliced water chestnuts
  ½ cup drained canned straw mushrooms or button mushrooms
  ½ cup drained, split, canned baby corn

1. Cut lobster into 1-inch chunks and butterfly-cut the shrimp (illustration, page 55)
2. Pat scallops dry and slice in half against the grain.
3. Mix marinade ingredients in a mixing bowl and add lobster, shrimp, and scallops, tossing to coat well. Cover and chill 1 hour minimum or overnight.
4. Mix 2 tablespoons oil into marinade to separate the pieces.
5. Mix seasonings.
6. Heat ½ cup of oil in a wok or skillet until very hot. Stir-fry seafood for 1 minute. Remove and drain well. Reserve oil.
7. Heat 1 tablespoon reserved oil in a wok or skillet over high heat. When oil is hot, add chili peppers, ginger, black beans, scallion, ham, black mushrooms, water chestnuts, straw mushrooms, and baby corn; cook, stirring, for 1 minute. Add seasonings, stirring constantly until sauce thickens and boils.
8. Return seafood and cook 30 seconds. Serve immediately.

TO PREPARE AHEAD: Follow steps 1–3; refrigerate. An hour before serving, follow steps 4–7. At last minute, reheat vegetables and follow step 8.

Makes 2–4 servings

PRAWNS IN SZECHUAN SAUCE
PAN LUNG TA HSIA ▪ Szechuan

1 pound prawns (20–25) or shrimp, shelled, deveined, washed, and
  patted dry
2 tablespoons peanut or other salad oil
1 cup peanut or other salad oil
2 cloves garlic, minced
1 tablespoon minced fresh ginger
¼ cup chopped onion
1 green pepper, seeded and ½-inch cubed
1 scallion, chopped, including stems

MARINADE:
  2 teaspoons cornstarch
  ½ teaspoon salt
  1 tablespoon rice wine or dry sherry
  1 small egg white

SEASONING SAUCE:
  2 tablespoons sugar
  2 tablespoons soy sauce
  2 tablespoons rice wine or dry sherry
  1½ tablespoons tomato paste
  ¼ cup chicken broth
  1 teaspoon hot-pepper oil (page 62)
  1 teaspoon cornstarch

1. Butterfly-cut the prawns (illustration, page 55).
2. Mix marinade and add prawns, tossing to coat. Cover and chill 1 hour minimum.
3. Mix seasonings.
4. Stir 2 tablespoons of oil into marinade to separate prawn pieces.
5. Heat 1 cup of oil in a wok or skillet until very hot. Stir-fry prawns 1 minute until pink and curled. Remove and drain. Reserve oil.
6. Heat 1 tablespoon reserved oil in a wok or skillet over high heat. Add garlic, ginger, onion, and scallion; stir-fry 1 minute. Add seasoning sauce, stirring constantly until it thickens and boils.
7. Add green pepper and scallion and bring to a boil. Return prawns and mix well. Serve immediately.

TO PREPARE AHEAD: Follow steps 1–3; refrigerate. Before serving, follow steps 4–6. To complete, follow step 7.

Makes 2–4 servings

SHRIMP WITH LOBSTER SAUCE
LUNG HSIA HU ▪ Canton

龍蝦糊

1 pound medium shrimp, shelled, deveined, washed, and patted dry
2 tablespoons peanut or other salad oil
2 teaspoons washed and crushed salted black beans
2 cloves garlic, minced
4 ounces ground pork
2 ounces lobster tail, shelled and chopped (optional)
3 tablespoons cornstarch dissolved in 3 tablespoons cold water
2 egg whites, slightly beaten
1 scallion, chopped, including stems

SEASONING SAUCE:
1 tablespoon rice wine or dry sherry
1 tablespoon soy sauce
1 teaspoon salt
½ teaspoon sugar
1 teaspoon sesame-seed oil
1 cup hot chicken broth

1. Butterfly-cut the shrimp (illustration, page 55).
2. Mix seasoning sauce.
3. Heat 2 tablespoons of oil in a wok or skillet over high heat until warm. Add black beans and garlic and stir-fry 15 seconds. Add pork and stir-fry 1 minute.
4. Add chopped lobster (optional) and shrimp; stir-fry about 30 seconds until shrimp turns pink.
5. Blend in seasoning sauce; bring to a boil and add dissolved cornstarch, stirring constantly until sauce thickens. Slowly drizzle in egg whites through chopsticks or fork and push gently. Cook 10 seconds and remove from heat as soon as egg whites begin to set. Sprinkle with scallion and serve immediately.

TO PREPARE AHEAD: Follow steps 1–3. Before serving, follow steps 4 and 5.

Makes 2–4 servings

STIR-FRIED PRAWN AND CHICKEN

YU LUNG SI FENG ▪ Canton

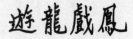

½ pound medium prawns or shrimp, shelled, deveined, washed, and
   patted dry
1 whole chicken breast
2 tablespoons peanut or other salad oil
½ cup peanut or other salad oil
½ cup sliced bamboo shoots
½ cup sliced carrots
⅓ pound snow peas
¼ cup toasted cashews or other nuts

MARINADE FOR SHRIMP AND CHICKEN:
½ teaspoon salt
1 tablespoon cornstarch dissolved in 1 tablespoon rice wine or dry sherry
½ egg white

SEASONING SAUCE:
1 clove garlic, chopped
1 teaspoon salt
1 teaspoon vinegar
1 teaspoon sugar
1 teaspoon sesame-seed oil
2 teaspoons cornstarch
2 tablespoons soy sauce
Dash of white pepper
⅓ cup chicken broth

1. Butterfly-cut the prawns (illustration, page 55).
2. Skin and bone chicken; cut into ¾-inch cubes.
3. Mix marinade and add prawns and chicken, tossing to coat. Cover and chill marinade 1 hour.
4. Mix seasonings.
5. Add 2 tablespoons of oil to marinade and mix well to separate pieces of prawns and chicken.
6. Heat ½ cup of oil to 400 degrees in a wok or skillet. Stir-fry prawns and chicken 2 minutes; do not overcook. Remove and drain. Reserve oil.
7. Heat 1 tablespoon reserved oil in a wok or skillet over high heat. Add bamboo shoots, carrots, and snow peas; stir-fry 1 minute. Return prawns and chicken, mix well. Add seasonings, stirring constantly until sauce thickens. Serve hot, sprinkled with cashews.

TO PREPARE AHEAD: Follow steps 1–4; refrigerate. Before serving, follow steps 5–7.

Makes 2–4 servings

STIR-FRIED SHRIMP WITH
GREEN PEAS
CHAO HSIA JEN ▪ Peking　　　　　　炒蝦仁

1 pound medium shrimp, shelled, deveined, washed, and patted dry
1 tablespoon peanut or other salad oil
½ cup peanut or other salad oil
1 10-ounce box of frozen peas, thawed
1 scallion, chopped, including stems
2 teaspoons washed and crushed salted black beans
½ teaspoon salt
½ teaspoon sugar
½ cup chicken broth or cold water
2 teaspoons cornstarch dissolved in 2 tablespoons cold water

MARINADE:
3 tablespoons rice wine or dry sherry
1¼ teaspoons salt
¼ teaspoon baking soda
2 tablespoons cornstarch
Dash of pepper

1. Butterfly-cut the shrimp (illustration, page 55).
2. Mix marinade and add shrimp, tossing to coat well. Cover and chill 2 hours minimum or overnight.
3. Mix 1 tablespoon of oil into marinade to separate shrimp.
4. Heat ½ cup of oil in a wok or skillet over high heat. Stir-fry shrimp 1 minute, until pink. Remove and drain. Reserve oil.
5. Heat reserved tablespoon oil over high heat. Add peas, scallion, black beans, salt, and sugar; stir-fry 30 seconds. Add chicken broth or water and bring to a boil. Add dissolved cornstarch, stirring constantly until sauce thickens and boils. Return shrimp and mix well. Serve immediately.

TO PREPARE AHEAD: Follow steps 1–3; refrigerate. Before serving, follow steps 4 and 5.

Makes 2–4 servings

SEAFOOD DELIGHT
CHAO HAI SIEN ▪ Peking

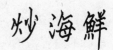

1 whole chicken breast, skinned and boned
4 ounces medium shrimp, shelled, deveined, washed, and patted dry
4 ounces bay scallops, washed and patted dry
2 tablespoons peanut or other salad oil
½ cup peanut or other salad oil

MARINADE:
1 tablespoon cornstarch
1 teaspoon salt
2 tablespoons rice wine or dry sherry

SEASONING SAUCE:
¾ teaspoon salt
¼ teaspoon white pepper
1 teaspoon cornstarch
1 teaspoon sesame-seed oil
½ cup chicken broth

SAUCE:
1 tablespoon peanut or other salad oil
1 teaspoon minced fresh ginger
1 clove garlic, minced
1 scallion, chopped, including stems
½ cup sliced water chestnuts
½ cup well-drained canned straw mushrooms or button mushrooms
½ cup drained, split, canned baby corn
1 cup 1-inch diagonally cut celery
2 ounces snow peas

1. Cut the chicken into ½-inch cubes; butterfly-cut the shrimp (illustration, page 55).

2. Mix the marinade and add chicken, shrimp, and scallops, tossing to coat well. Cover and chill 1 hour.

3. Mix seasoning sauce.

4. Add 2 tablespoons of oil to marinade, stirring well to separate pieces of chicken, shrimp, and scallops.

5. Heat ½ cup of oil in a wok or skillet until very hot. Stir-fry chicken, shrimp, and scallops 1 minute. Remove and drain well. Reserve oil.

6. Heat 1 tablespoon reserved oil over high heat. Add ginger, garlic, and scallion; stir-fry 30 seconds. Add water chestnuts, mushrooms, baby corn, and celery; stir-fry 1 minute. Add seasoning sauce, stir constantly until sauce thickens and boils.

7. Add snow peas; return chicken, shrimp, and scallops. Mix well. Serve hot.

TO PREPARE AHEAD: Follow steps 1–3; refrigerate. Before serving, follow steps 4–6. At last minute, reheat sauce and follow step 7.

Makes 2–4 servings

STUFFED SHRIMP
NIANG TA HSIA ▪ Canton

½ cup ginger sauce (page 64)
16 large shrimp (about 1 pound), shelled, deveined, and washed
Peanut or other salad oil for deep-frying

COATING:
  2 tablespoons all-purpose flour
  1 egg, well-beaten
  1 cup fine dried breadcrumbs

FILLING:
  5 ounces fresh crab meat, flaked and cartilage removed
  2 scallions, chopped, including stems
  ½ cup chopped and packed bamboo shoots
  1 teaspoon minced fresh ginger root
  ⅛ teaspoon white pepper
  1 teaspoon sugar
  ¾ teaspoon salt
  1 teaspoon sesame-seed oil
  ½ egg, slightly beaten
  1 tablespoon cornstarch dissolved in 1 tablespoon rice wine or dry sherry

  1. Prepare ginger sauce.
  2. Butterfly-cut the shrimp (illustration, page 55), and dredge in flour.
  3. Mix filling ingredients.
  4. Spread shrimp with filling, dip into beaten egg and coat with bread-crumbs.
  5. Heat 1 inch of oil to 325 degrees in a wok or skillet over medium heat. Fry shrimp, stuffed-side down, 2–3 minutes; turn and cook 1 minute longer or until golden brown. Pierce filling with a fork; if no liquid escapes, the shrimp is done. Serve with ginger sauce.

TO PREPARE AHEAD: Follow steps 1–5; refrigerate or freeze. Before serving, reheat on a rack 10 minutes in preheated 400-degree oven until hot and crispy.

Makes 4 servings

BAKED WHOLE FISH
K'AO YU ■ National

1 fresh whole yellow pike (or flounder, trout, whitefish, or striped bass),
   about 2 pounds
2½ teaspoons salt
1 tablespoon peanut or other salad oil
2 scallions, shredded, including stems
1 clove garlic, minced
1 teaspoon shredded fresh ginger
2 strips bacon, shredded
⅓ cup shredded bamboo shoots
⅓ cup shredded cooked ham
2 dried Chinese black mushrooms, soaked in hot water 20 minutes,
   stemmed and sliced
2 tablespoons soy sauce
2 tablespoons rice wine or dry sherry
½ teaspoon sugar
2 teaspoons sesame-seed oil

1. Clean and scale fish (leave on head and tail). Rub fish with 2 teaspoons salt; set aside 10 minutes. Wash with water; dry with paper towels inside and out. Score diagonally, almost to the bone, on both sides, about 2 inches apart.

2. Line a large, shallow baking pan about 4″ longer than the fish with a large piece of heavy-duty aluminum foil. Grease foil with 1 tablespoon of oil and center fish in the pan.

3. Combine scallion, garlic, ginger, bacon, bamboo shoots, ham, mushrooms, soy sauce, sherry, sugar, sesame-seed oil, and remaining ½ teaspoon salt.

4. Stuff mixture into incisions on both sides of fish and close foil loosely over fish.

5. Bake in preheated 450-degree oven 20–25 minutes. (For fish over 2 pounds, allow 5–8 minutes extra per pound.)

6. Transfer carefully to a heated serving platter, drench with pan juices and serve immediately.

TO PREPARE AHEAD: Follow steps 1–4; refrigerate. A half-hour before serving, follow steps 5 and 6.

Makes 2–4 servings

PINEAPPLE FISH
PO LO YU ▪ Canton

1 pound sole or flounder fillet
Peanut or other salad oil for deep-frying

MARINADE:
⅓ teaspoon salt
1 tablespoon rice wine or dry sherry
⅛ teaspoon white pepper
1 egg

COATING:
½ cup cornstarch
½ cup flour

PINEAPPLE SAUCE:
1 tablespoon peanut or other salad oil
1 clove garlic, minced
1 teaspoon shredded ginger root
⅓ cup packed brown sugar
⅓ cup cider vinegar
1 tablespoon soy sauce
½ cup syrup from canned pineapple
½ cup water
1½ tablespoons cornstarch dissolved in 4 tablespoons cold water
½ cup drained canned pineapple chunks
2 tablespoons sliced toasted almonds

1. Cut fish fillet into diagonal pieces about 1 × 2 inches.
2. Mix marinade and add fish, tossing to coat. Cover and chill 10 minutes.
3. Mix ½ cup cornstarch and ½ cup flour in plastic bag. Add fish, a few pieces at a time; shake to coat well. Remove to a flour-dusted cookie sheet; do not stack on top of each other.
4. Heat 1 inch of oil in a wok or skillet until very hot. Fry fish on both sides until light brown. Drain well. Arrange fish on platter and hold in 200-degree oven.
5. Heat 1 tablespoon oil over high heat; lightly brown the garlic and ginger. Blend in brown sugar, vinegar, soy sauce, pineapple syrup, and water; bring to a boil. Add dissolved cornstarch, stirring constantly until sauce thickens and boils. Mix in pineapple chunks. Pour sauce over fish and sprinkle with sliced almonds. Serve immediately.

TO PREPARE AHEAD: Follow steps 1–4, frying fish to very light brown and follow step 5 to make sauce several hours before serving. When serving, fry fish again until light brown, or place fish on a rack in a foil-lined baking pan. Reheat 5–10 minutes in a preheated 400-degree oven. Pour sauce over fish and sprinkle with sliced almonds.

Makes 2–4 servings

ROSE FISH BALL

CHIEH CHIH YU CHIU ■ **Shanghai**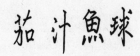

1 pound fish fillet, skin on (sea bass, yellow pike, or perch)
1 cup peas
Peanut or other salad oil for deep-frying

BATTER:
1 teaspoon minced fresh ginger
½ teaspoon salt
1 tablespoon rice wine or dry sherry
1 egg white
3 tablespoons cornstarch
3 tablespoons all-purpose flour

SEASONING SAUCE:
1 dried chili pepper, chopped
½ teaspoon salt
2 tablespoons soy sauce
2 tablespoons sugar
2 tablespoons cider vinegar
2 teaspoons cornstarch
1 tablespoon tomato paste
½ cup cold water

1. Wash and dry the fillets; score ⅓-inch deep on the meat side; cut in 1½-inch squares.
2. Combine the batter in a mixing bowl until free of lumps. Add fish fillet and mix well. Allow the fish to sit in batter for 10 minutes in the refrigerator.
3. Mix seasoning sauce.
4. Heat 3 inches of oil to 375 degrees in a wok or large saucepan over high heat. Fry each fillet until golden brown. Remove and drain well.
5. Mix seasoning sauce in wok or saucepan. Cook, stirring constantly until sauce thickens.
6. Add peas and bring to a boil. Return fish and mix well. Serve immediately.

TO PREPARE AHEAD: Follow steps 1–4; refrigerate. Before serving, re-fry until crispy or reheat 10–15 minutes in a preheated 350-degree oven; follow steps 5 and 6.

Makes 2–4 servings

SESAME FISH
CHIH MA YU ■ Canton

芝蔴魚

1 pound fish fillet (sole or flounder)
¼ cup flour
1 egg, well beaten
¼ cup sesame seeds
⅔ cup fine dried breadcrumbs
Peanut or other salad oil for frying

MARINADE:
1 clove garlic, minced
1 tablespoon minced fresh ginger
1 scallion, minced, including stems
½ teaspoon salt
¼ teaspoon white pepper
2 tablespoons rice wine or dry sherry
1 tablespoon lemon juice

DIPPING SAUCE:
2 tablespoons sugar
1 tablespoon cider vinegar
¼ cup soy sauce
1 teaspoon hot-pepper oil
1 teaspoon sesame-seed oil

1. Wash the fish and pat dry; cut into 2 × 3-inch pieces.
2. Mix marinade and add fish, tossing to coat. Cover and chill 1 hour.
3. Mix sesame seeds and breadcrumbs.
4. Mix dipping sauce.
5. Coat fish lightly with flour, tossing in a plastic bag.
6. Dip coated fish in egg; coat both sides lightly in sesame-breadcrumb mixture.
7. Heat ½ inch of oil to 375 degrees in a wok or skillet. Fry fish until golden brown on both sides. Serve immediately with dipping sauce.

TO PREPARE AHEAD: Follow steps 1–7, frying fish light brown only; refrigerate. Before serving, re-fry to golden brown.

Makes 2–4 servings

SCALLOPS CANTONESE
CH'AO KAO PEI ▪ Canton

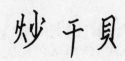

1 pound scallops, cut in half crosswise
4 tablespoons peanut or other salad oil
½ cup sliced bamboo shoots
½ cup sliced water chestnuts
½ cup 1-inch diagonally cut chunks Chinese cabbage
1 small onion, 1-inch cubed
3 dried Chinese black mushrooms, soaked in hot water 20 minutes,
   stemmed and quartered
1 teaspoon salt
1 teaspoon soy sauce
1 cup chicken broth or water
1 tablespoon cornstarch dissolved in 3 tablespoons cold water
½ cup blanched almonds, toasted or fried

MARINADE:
1 clove garlic, chopped
1 teaspoon minced fresh ginger
½ teaspoon salt
1 tablespoon rice wine or dry sherry
½ teaspoon sugar

1. Mix marinade and add scallops, tossing to coat well. Cover and chill 15 minutes.

2. Heat 3 tablespoons oil in a wok or skillet over medium heat. Stir-fry almonds until light brown. Remove and drain. Increase heat; when oil is very hot, stir-fry scallops 2 minutes. Remove and set aside.

3. Heat remaining tablespoon of oil in a wok or skillet over high heat. Add bamboo shoots, water chestnuts, cabbage, onion, and Chinese mushrooms; stir-fry 2 minutes. Add salt, soy sauce, and chicken broth; bring to a boil. Add dissolved cornstarch, stirring constantly until sauce thickens and boils. Return scallops and mix well. Sprinkle with almonds and serve hot.

TO PREPARE AHEAD: Mix marinade and cut ingredients ahead of time; refrigerate. Before serving, marinate scallops and follow steps 2 and 3.

Makes 2–4 servings

LOBSTER CANTONESE
CH'AO LUNG HSIA ▪ Canton

炒 龍 蝦

2 whole live lobsters or 1 pound frozen lobster tails
2 tablespoons peanut or other salad oil
1 tablespoon washed and crushed salted black beans
2 cloves garlic, minced
1 teaspoon minced fresh ginger
¼ pound ground pork
1 cup boiling water
2 tablespoons cornstarch dissolved in 3 tablespoons cold water
2 egg whites, slightly beaten
2 scallions, chopped, including stems

SEASONING SAUCE:
1 tablespoon rice wine or dry sherry
2 tablespoons soy sauce
½ teaspoon salt
½ teaspoon sugar
1 teaspoon sesame-seed oil

1. Wash lobster, split lengthwise and cut into bite-sized pieces. (Lobster may be cut while still frozen.)
2. Mix seasoning sauce.
3. Heat 2 tablespoons oil until warm in a wok or skillet over high heat. Add black beans, garlic, and ginger root; stir-fry 30 seconds. Add pork, stir-fry 2 minutes.
4. Add lobster; stir-fry 2 minutes until pink.
5. Blend in 1 cup boiling water and seasoning sauce. Bring to a boil; add dissolved cornstarch and stir constantly until sauce thickens and boils. Drizzle in egg whites through chopsticks or fork and push gently until lightly set (about 30 seconds). Remove from heat immediately. Mix in scallions and serve immediately.

TO PREPARE AHEAD: Follow steps 1–3 an hour before serving. To complete, follow steps 4 and 5.

Makes 2–4 servings

VEGETABLES, SALAD, AND BEAN CURD

蔬菜豆腐

BUDDHA DELIGHT
LO HAN CHAI ■ Canton

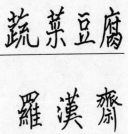

羅漢齋

2 tablespoons peanut or other salad oil
5 dried Chinese black mushrooms, soaked in hot water 20 minutes,
    stemmed and halved
½ cup sliced bamboo shoots
½ cup sliced water chestnuts
½ cup drained, split, canned baby corn
½ cup drained, canned straw mushrooms or fresh mushrooms
½ cup sliced carrots
¼ pound fresh snow peas

SEASONING SAUCE:
1 scallion, chopped, including stems
1 tablespoon oyster sauce
1 teaspoon salt
1 teaspoon sugar
1 teaspoon sesame-seed oil
½ cup chicken broth
2 teaspoons cornstarch

1. Mix seasoning sauce.
2. Heat oil in wok or skillet until very hot. Add all vegetables and stir-fry
2 minutes. Add seasoning sauce, stirring constantly until it thickens and
boils. Serve hot.

TO PREPARE AHEAD: Follow steps 1 and 2, omitting snow peas. Refrigerate. Before serving, reheat, adding snow peas at last minute.

Makes 2–4 servings

HOT-AND-SOUR MUSHROOMS
SUAN LA YUNG KU ▪ Canton

酸 辣 洋 菇

1½ pounds fresh mushrooms
1 cup fine dried breadcrumbs
Peanut or other salad oil for deep-frying
1 tablespoon peanut or other salad oil

HOT AND SOUR SAUCE:
1 tablespoon peanut oil
1 clove garlic, minced
2 dried chili peppers, chopped
1 medium onion, 1-inch cubed
1 carrot, peeled and diagonally cut in 1-inch pieces
⅓ cup cider vinegar
⅓ cup sugar
¼ cup syrup from canned pineapple
⅓ cup water
1 tablespoon cornstarch dissolved in ¼ cup cold water
½ cup drained pineapple chunks (reserve syrup)

BATTER:
1 egg
¼ cup water
3 tablespoons cornstarch
3 tablespoons sweet rice flour
1 teaspoon salt

1. Wash the mushrooms; drain, pat dry and trim ¼-inch off stems.
2. Combine batter ingredients; mix well until free of lumps.
3. Dip mushrooms into batter and coat lightly with breadcrumbs.
4. Heat 2 inches of oil to 375 degrees in a wok or deep-fryer. Fry mushrooms until light brown; drain. (At this point the mushrooms can be served as an hors d'oeuvre.)
5. Heat 1 tablespoon oil in wok or skillet over high heat. Add garlic, chili, onion, and carrot; stir-fry 1 minute. Add vinegar, sugar, pineapple syrup, and water; bring to a boil. Add dissolved cornstarch, stirring constantly until sauce thickens and boils.
6. Add pineapple chunks and fried mushrooms. Mix well and serve immediately.

TO PREPARE AHEAD: Follow steps 1–5. Before serving, re-fry the mushrooms briefly and reheat the sauce; then follow step 6.

Makes 2–4 servings

STIR-FRIED ASPARAGUS
WITH PORK
LU SUN CHU RUH ■ National

蘆筍豬肉

¾ pound pork tenderloin or lean pork
1 pound fresh asparagus
3 tablespoons peanut or other salad oil
1 clove garlic, minced
½ teaspoon salt
1 scallion, chopped, including stems
1 tablespoon rice wine or dry sherry

MARINADE:
1 tablespoon soy sauce
¼ teaspoon salt
½ teaspoon sugar
1 teaspoon sesame-seed oil
1 teaspoon cornstarch dissolved in 1 tablespoon water

1. Slice the pork ⅛-inch thick and julienne.
2. Mix marinade and add pork, tossing to coat. Cover and chill 15 minutes.
3. Wash asparagus; discard scales and woody ends. Slice diagonally ¼-inch thick.
4. Heat oil in a wok or skillet until very hot. Stir-fry pork 1 minute. Add asparagus, garlic, salt, scallion, and rice wine; stir-fry 3 minutes. Serve hot.

TO PREPARE AHEAD: Follow steps 1–3; refrigerate. Before serving follow step 4.

Makes 2–4 servings

STIR-FRIED CAULIFLOWER
AND MUSHROOMS
TUNG KU TSAI HUA ▪ National

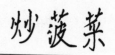

2 tablespoons peanut or other salad oil
2 cloves garlic, minced
1 scallion, chopped, including stems
1¼ teaspoons salt
1½ pounds cauliflower, cut into bite-sized pieces
5 dried Chinese black mushrooms, soaked in hot water 15 minutes,
  stemmed, and halved
½ cup sliced carrots
¾ cup chicken broth

1. Heat 2 tablespoons oil in a wok or skillet until very hot. Add garlic, scallion, and salt; stir-fry 10 seconds.
2. Add cauliflower, mushrooms, carrots, and chicken broth; cover and cook over medium heat 5–8 minutes, stirring occasionally, until the cauliflower is crisp-tender. Serve hot.

TO PREPARE AHEAD: Follow steps 1 and 2, undercooking cauliflower. To complete, cook until cauliflower is crisp-tender.

Makes 2–4 servings

STIR-FRIED SPINACH
CH'AO PO TS'AI ▪ National

炒菠菜

1 pound fresh spinach or 1 10-ounce package pre-washed spinach
2 tablespoons peanut or other salad oil
1 clove garlic, chopped
½ teaspoon salt
2 tablespoons slivered almonds, toasted

1. Wash and drain spinach, removing any wilted leaves.
2. Heat oil in a wok or skillet until very hot. Add garlic, salt, and spinach; stir-fry until spinach wilts. Sprinkle with almonds and serve immediately on heated platter.

Makes 2–3 servings

STUFFED CUCUMBER
SIANG HUANG KUA ▪ Canton

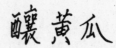

3 large cucumbers
Flour for dusting
1 cup chicken broth
¾ teaspoon salt

FILLING:
½ pound ground pork, beef, veal, or chicken
1 tablespoon soy sauce
¾ teaspoon salt
1 tablespoon rice wine or dry sherry
1 scallion, minced, including stems
2 tablespoons minced water chestnuts
1 teaspoon cornstarch dissolved in 1 tablespoon water
1 egg

SAUCE:
1 cup juice from steamed cucumbers, strained
1 teaspoon soy sauce
2½ teaspoons cornstarch dissolved in 2 tablespoons
cold water

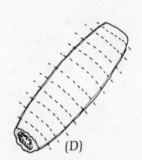

Making Stuffed Cucumbers

1. Peel cucumbers; trim and reserve the ends (a). Hollow out cucumbers, scooping out seeds with a long spoon. Dry insides with paper towels, then dust inside with flour.
2. Mix filling and stuff cucumbers, packing tightly (b).
3. Fasten ends of cucumbers with toothpicks.
4. Place cucumbers on a pie plate (c). Add 1 cup chicken broth and salt. Steam for 2 minutes, turning once, or until tender. Reserve juice for sauce.
5. Slice 1-inch thick slices (d) and keep warm on a serving platter.
6. Combine 1 cup reserved juice, soy sauce, and dissolved cornstarch; cook over low heat, stirring constantly until sauce thickens and boils. Pour over sliced cucumbers and serve hot.

TO PREPARE AHEAD: Follow steps 1–4, steaming 15 minutes only; refrigerate. Before serving, steam 10 minutes; follow steps 5 and 6.

Makes 4–6 servings

YU HSIANG EGGPLANT
YU HSIANG CHIEH TZU ▪ Szechuan

魚香茄子

2 eggplants, about 1 pound each
¼ pound ground beef or pork
Peanut or other salad oil for deep-frying
1 tablespoon peanut or other salad oil
2 dried chili peppers, chopped
1 tablespoon soybean paste
1 clove garlic, minced
1 scallion, minced, including stems
1 tablespoon soy sauce
¼ teaspoon salt
1 teaspoon sugar
1 teaspoon sesame-seed oil

MARINADE:
1 teaspoon cornstarch
1 tablespoon soy sauce
1 tablespoon rice wine or dry sherry

1. Cut the eggplants into quarters lengthwise and slice diagonally 1½-inches thick.

2. Mix marinade and add meat.

3. Heat 2–3″ oil to 375 degrees in a wok or deep-fryer. Fry eggplant 5 minutes until tender. Press gently to drain well.

4. Heat 1 tablespoon of oil in a wok or skillet until hot. Add chili peppers, bean paste, garlic, and scallion; stir-fry 15 seconds. Add the meat; stir-fry 2 minutes. Add eggplant, soy sauce, salt, sugar, and sesame-seed oil; stir-fry 2 minutes. Remove and serve hot.

TO PREPARE AHEAD: Follow steps 1–4. Before serving, reheat in a wok or covered in a 375-degree oven for 15 minutes.

Makes 2 servings

SHRIMP WITH CUCUMBER SALAD
HSIA JEN PAN HUANG KUA ■ Peking

蝦仁样黄瓜

1 pound large or medium shrimp
2 medium cucumbers
3 tablespoons crushed toasted sesame seeds

DRESSING:
1 clove garlic, minced
2 scallions, minced, including stems
1 tablespoon cider vinegar
3 tablespoons soy sauce
1 tablespoon sesame-seed oil
1 tablespoon hot-pepper oil (page 62)
1 tablespoon sugar
¼ teaspoon salt

1. Make hot-pepper oil.
2. Steam the shrimp in a single layer 8 minutes. Allow to cool; shell, devein, and split lengthwise.
3. Peel and split cucumbers; scoop out seeds. Slice halves crosswise ⅓-inch thick.
4. Center shrimp on serving platter; ring with sliced cucumber around the shrimp. Cover and chill.
5. Mix dressing and pour over salad. Serve cold.

TO PREPARE AHEAD: Follow steps 1–5, but chill dressing separately. Before serving, shake dressing well and pour over salad.

Makes 2–4 servings

SHIH CHIN SALAD
SHIH CHIN PAN TSAI ▪ Peking

什錦拌菜

1 whole chicken breast, cooked
4 slices boiled ham (about ⅓ pound)
2 egg skins (page 46)
1 cucumber
½ cup shredded carrots
2 cups julienned lettuce

DRESSING:

3 tablespoons soy sauce
3 tablespoons vinegar
1 teaspoon sugar
½ teaspoon salt
2 teaspoons sesame-seed oil
2 tablespoons toasted sesame seeds, crushed (page 41)

1. Make egg skins and toasted sesame seeds.
2. Shred the chicken, discarding bone and skin. Julienne ham and egg skins.
3. Peel cucumber and split lengthwise. Remove seeds; slice thinly.
4. Arrange chicken, ham, egg skins, cucumber, carrots, and lettuce in a circle on a serving platter.
5. Mix dressing ingredients except sesame seeds and pour over the salad. Sprinkle with sesame seeds immediately before serving.

TO PREPARE AHEAD: Follow steps 1–5, but chill salad and dressing separately. Add dressing and sesame seeds before serving.

Makes 2–4 servings

CRAB MEAT BEAN CURD
KUO TA TOU FU ■ Peking

鍋 塔 豆腐

1 pound bean curd, drained
½ cup flour
2 eggs, well beaten
Peanut or other salad oil for frying
4 tablespoons peanut or other salad oil
Hot-pepper oil sauce (page 62)

CRAB MEAT COATING:
¼ pound canned crab meat
2 scallions, minced, including stems
1½ teaspoons salt
2 tablespoons rice wine or dry sherry
3 eggs, well beaten

1. Make hot-pepper oil sauce.
2. Pick cartilage from crab meat.
3. Mix crab meat, scallions, salt, rice wine, and eggs.
4. Slice bean curd ½-inch thick and coat with flour.
5. Heat ¼-inch oil to 350 degrees in a skillet. Dip floured bean curd into beaten egg and fry until light brown on both sides. Remove and drain.
6. Heat 4 tablespoons of oil in skillet over medium heat. Arrange one layer fried bean cake in the pan and pour the crab meat mixture evenly over bean curd; cover and pan-fry 5–8 minutes until golden brown. Turn and fry other side until light brown. Serve hot with hot-pepper oil sauce.

TO PREPARE AHEAD: Follow steps 1–5; refrigerate. Before serving follow step 6.

Makes 2–4 servings

EIGHT-PRECIOUS BEAN CURD
PA CHEN TOU FU ■ Canton

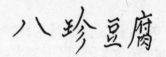

3 large eggs
2 tablespoons cornstarch
2 tablespoons rice wine or dry sherry
¼ cup chicken broth
¼ pound fillet of flounder or sole
1 pound bean curd
4 tablespoons rice flour
1½ teaspoons salt
½ teaspoon sugar
1 teaspoon sesame-seed oil
Dash of white pepper
2 ounces chopped fresh or cooked shrimp
½ cup cooked ham, chopped
1 cooked Chinese sausage (see note) or Italian sausage (2 ounces),
 chopped
1 scallion, minced, including stems
Peanut or other salad oil for deep-frying
½ cup plum sauce or ginger sauce (page 64)

COATING:
1 cup breadcrumbs
2 tablespoons sesame seeds
1 egg, well beaten

1. Make plum or ginger sauce.
2. Put the eggs, cornstarch, rice wine, chicken broth, and flounder in a blender and blend 1 minute. Add bean curd piece by piece; blend well.
3. Remove mixture to a bowl; mix in rice flour, salt, sugar, sesame-seed oil, white pepper, shrimp, ham, sausage, and scallion.
4. Pour into well-greased 10-inch pie plate and steam 10 minutes. Allow to cool; turn out and cut into 1 × 1½ inches.
5. Mix breadcrumbs and sesame seeds. Dip bean curd pieces into beaten egg and then coat with mixture.
6. Heat 2 inches of oil to 375 degrees in a wok or a deep-fryer. Fry coated bean curd until golden brown. Serve hot with plum or ginger sauce.

NOTE: To cook Chinese sausage, steam 30 minutes.

TO PREPARE AHEAD: Follow steps 1–6, frying to light brown only. Before serving, re-fry until golden brown.

Makes 2–4 servings

POCKET BEAN CURD
KOU TAI TOU FU ▪ Szechuan

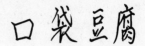

1 pound bean curd
½ chicken breast, skinned, boned, and minced
1 scallion, minced, including stems
1 tablespoon rice wine or dry sherry
1 tablespoon cornstarch
1 teaspoon salt
Dash of white pepper
3 egg whites
Peanut or other salad oil for deep-frying

SAUCE:
1 cup chicken broth
1 teaspoon salt
1 can (15 ounces) straw mushrooms, drained, or ½ pound fresh
   mushrooms, halved
1 tablespoon cornstarch dissolved in ¼ cup cold water
1 teaspoon sesame-seed oil
2 tablespoons chopped cooked ham

1. Place bean curd in blender, piece by piece, and reduce to paste.
2. Combine bean-curd paste with chicken, scallion, rice wine, cornstarch, salt, and white pepper.
3. Beat egg whites until stiff; fold into bean-curd mixture.
4. Heat 2–3 inches of oil to 375 degrees in a wok or deep-fryer. Deep-fry bean-curd mixture, one tablespoon at a time, until light brown. Drain.
5. Heat chicken broth in a wok or skillet. Add salt and mushrooms; cook 1 minute. Add dissolved cornstarch, stirring constantly until sauce thickens and boils.
6. Fold fried bean curd and sesame-seed oil into sauce; bring to a boil. Remove to a platter and serve hot, sprinkled with chopped ham.

TO PREPARE AHEAD: Follow steps 1–5, cover, and refrigerate. Before serving, follow step 6.

Makes 2–4 servings

SOUPS

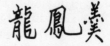

DRAGON-AND-PHOENIX SOUP
LUNG FENG KENG ▪ Peking

1 whole chicken breast
¼ pound shrimp or king crab meat, chopped
3 egg whites
1 teaspoon white pepper
1 teaspoon salt
1 tablespoon sesame-seed oil

SOUP:
6 cups chicken broth
2¼ teaspoons salt
1 teaspoon sugar
4 tablespoons cornstarch dissolved in 1 cup cold water
2 scallions, minced, including stems

1. Skin, bone, and mince the chicken breast.
2. Mix with shrimp, egg whites, white pepper, salt, and sesame-seed oil; cover and chill 90 minutes.
3. Boil chicken broth; add salt and sugar. Add dissolved cornstarch; stir constantly until sauce thickens and boils.
4. Stir 1 cup hot soup into chicken mixture to smooth it; then stir chicken mixture into soup. Bring to boil; then remove from heat, add scallions, and serve.

TO PREPARE AHEAD: Follow step 1; refrigerate. Before serving, follow steps 2–4.

Makes 6 servings

FISH-FILLET SOUP
YU SHENG TANG ▪ Hunan

½ pound fresh fish fillet (striped bass, yellow pike, or sole)
1 tablespoon rice wine or dry sherry
½ teaspoon salt
2 cups peanut or other salad oil
3 ounces dried Chinese instant noodles
2 tablespoons minced roasted peanuts
2 tablespoons crushed toasted sesame seeds
2 tablespoons minced scallion
2 tablespoons minced parsley
1 cup shredded fresh spinach leaves
1½ teaspoons salt
1 teaspoon sesame-seed oil
Dash of pepper
6 cups chicken broth

1. Cut the fish into paper-thin slices; mix with 1 tablespoon rice wine and ½ teaspoon salt. Cover and chill 10 minutes.

2. Heat 2 cups oil over medium heat. Add noodles; deep-fry until golden brown. Drain well; break into 1-inch pieces.

3. Cover bottom of tureen with noodles. Lay fish on noodles; sprinkle with peanuts, crushed sesame seeds, scallion, parsley, spinach, salt, sesame-seed oil, and pepper.

4. Bring chicken broth to a boil and pour boiling broth over fish. Cover, let rest 1 minute and serve.

TO PREPARE AHEAD: Follow steps 1–3; refrigerate. Before serving, follow step 4 but let rest 3 minutes.

Makes 6 servings

HOT-AND-SOUR SOUP
SUAN LA T'ANG ▪ Peking

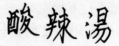

5½ cups chicken broth
⅓ pound julienned lean pork
½ cup julienned cooked ham
½ cup shredded bamboo shoots
20 dried tiger lily buds, soaked in hot water 10 minutes, stemmed, and
   cut in half crosswise
4 dried Chinese black mushrooms, soaked in hot water 15 minutes,
   stemmed, and thinly sliced
2 tablespoons dried wood ears, soaked in warm water for 10 minutes,
   washed, and julienned
½ cup julienned bean curd
3 tablespoons soy sauce
¼ cup cider vinegar
1¼ teaspoons white pepper
1¼ teaspoons salt
1 teaspoon sesame-seed oil
5 tablespoons cornstarch dissolved in 1 cup cold water
2 eggs, slightly beaten
1 scallion, chopped, including stems

1. Bring the chicken broth to a boil in a large saucepan. Add pork, ham,
bamboo shoots, tiger lily buds, Chinese mushrooms, wood ears, and bean
curd; simmer 3 minutes.

2. Add soy sauce, vinegar, white pepper, salt, and sesame-seed oil; bring
to a boil. Add dissolved cornstarch, stirring constantly until soup thickens
and boils. Drizzle in the beaten egg through chopsticks or a fork and push
gently until egg is slightly set. Turn off heat, sprinkle with scallion and serve
hot.

TO PREPARE AHEAD: Follow step 1 and allow to cool. Before serving, follow step 2.

Makes 4–6 servings

MEATBALLS WITH
BEAN-THREAD SOUP
FEN SSU ROW WAN T'ANG ▪ Peking

粉絲肉圓湯

MEATBALLS:
½ pound ground lean pork
¼ teaspoon salt
¼ teaspoon sugar
2 tablespoons soy sauce
1 teaspoon sesame-seed oil
1 tablespoon rice wine or dry sherry
2 teaspoons cornstarch dissolved in 4 tablespoons cold water
Dash of pepper
1 scallion, minced, including stems

SOUP:
2 ounces bean threads
6 cups chicken broth
1½ teaspoons salt or to taste
2 tablespoons finely chopped Szechuan pickles (optional)

   1. Mix meatball ingredients and roll into 1½-inch ovals. Place on a wet plate.
   2. Soak bean threads in warm water 5 minutes or until soft. Drain and cut into 2-inch bits.
   3. Bring chicken broth to a boil. Add salt and meatballs; return to boil and cook 3 minutes over medium heat. Skim excess fat.
   4. Add bean threads and cook 1 minute. Remove from heat; sprinkle with pickles and serve.

TO PREPARE AHEAD: Follow steps 1 and 2; refrigerate. Before serving, follow steps 3 and 4.

Makes 6–8 servings

PORK-AND-CUCUMBER SOUP
CHU ROW HUANG KUA T'ANG ▪ Peking

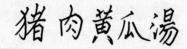

⅓ pound lean pork
1 large cucumber
6 cups chicken or beef broth
2 teaspoons salt
Dash of pepper

MARINADE:
1 teaspoon cornstarch
2 teaspoons soy sauce
1 tablespoon rice wine or dry sherry

1. Cut pork into 1 × 2-inch strips with the grain; slice paper-thin.
2. Mix marinade and add pork, tossing to coat. Cover and chill 10 minutes.
3. Peel and split cucumber; scoop out seeds; slice ⅛-inch thick.
4. Bring chicken broth to a boil. Add pork and cucumber; cover and cook for 2–3 minutes. Skim; add salt and pepper. Serve hot.

VARIATION: Beef or veal replace pork. Cook cucumber until tender before adding beef or veal. Bring to a boil; serve at once.

TO PREPARE AHEAD: Follow steps 1–4; reheat before serving.

Makes 4–6 servings

SHIH CHIN SOUP
SHIH CHIN TANG ▪ Shantung

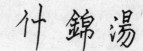

½ whole chicken breast, skinned, boned, and sliced paper-thin
¼ pound julienned lean pork
½ cup julienned cooked ham
1 cup julienned bean curd
1 egg skin (page 46), julienned
3 dried Chinese black mushrooms, soaked in hot water 15 minutes,
    stemmed, and sliced

SOUP:
6 cups chicken broth
2 tablespoons soy sauce
2 teaspoons salt
½ teaspoon white pepper
1 teaspoon sesame-seed oil
4 tablespoons cornstarch dissolved in ½ cup cold water
2 eggs, well beaten
1 scallion, minced, including stems
¼ cup minced parsley

1. Heat the chicken broth, add soy sauce, salt, white pepper, and sesame-seed oil, and bring to a boil. Add chicken, pork, ham, bean curd, egg skin, and mushrooms; return to boil again. Add dissolved cornstarch, stirring constantly until soup thickens and boils.

2. Slowly drizzle in the beaten egg through chopsticks or a fork. Push twice gently until the egg is set slightly; remove from heat. Sprinkle with scallion and parsley, and serve hot.

TO PREPARE AHEAD: Follow steps 1 and 2 an hour before serving, and keep hot.

Makes 4–6 servings

TOMATO-FLOWER SOUP
FAN CH'IEH T'ANG ▪ National

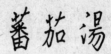

1 pound fresh tomatoes
1 tablespoon peanut or other salad oil
1 scallion, chopped, including stems
1 tablespoon peanut or other salad oil
5 cups chicken or beef broth
1½ teaspoons salt
2 eggs slightly beaten
Dash of pepper

1. Peel tomatoes (see note). Cut in half crosswise. (Do not cut lengthwise.) Remove seeds. Cut into 1-inch wedges.

2. Heat oil in a wok or saucepan until very hot. Add tomato wedges and scallion; stir-fry 1 minute. Add broth and salt. Bring to a boil and slowly drizzle egg through chopsticks or fork into soup. When egg is lightly set (about 30 seconds), add pepper and serve.

NOTE: To peel tomatoes: Insert fork into tomato and dip in boiling water 30 seconds, or hold over gas flame 30 seconds. Then peel.

TO PREPARE AHEAD: Follow steps 1 and 2, but omit broth and egg. Refrigerate. Before serving, add boiling broth, bring soup to a boil. Drizzle in egg and serve immediately.

Makes 4–6 servings

WONTON SOUP
HUN TUN T'ANG ▪ National

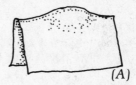

40 wonton wrappers

FILLING:
- ½ pound ground chuck or pork or chicken or shrimp
- 2 tablespoons soy sauce
- 1 tablespoon rice wine or dry sherry
- ½ teaspoon salt
- ¼ teaspoon sugar
- 1 teaspoon sesame-seed oil
- 1 egg
- 2 scallions, minced, including stems
- ¼ cup minced bamboo shoots
- Dash of pepper

SOUP:
- 6 cups chicken or beef broth
- 2 tablespoons soy sauce
- 2 teaspoons salt
- 1 scallion, minced, including stems

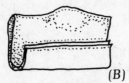

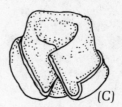

Making Wontons for Wonton Soup

1. Mix filling.

2. Moisten wonton wrappers on one side and cover with damp cloth. Place 1 teaspoon filling in the center of each wrapper. Fold over at the center (a). Wet with water along the edges and press together. Fold in ⅓ lengthwise at the open side (b). Bring the two ends over the other and press together with a little water (c).

3. Boil 3 quarts water. Add wontons, stirring constantly. Cover and return to boil. Add 1 cup cold water; cover and return to boil. When wontons are cooked, they will float. Drain and rinse with cold water to stop cooking.

4. Boil chicken broth with soy sauce, and salt. Add wontons and return to boil. Sprinkle with scallion and serve hot.

NOTE: When using pork filling, cook longer in step 3: Add 2 cups cold water and return to boil.

TO PREPARE AHEAD: Follow steps 1 and 2; freeze in single layer on lightly floured tray. Before serving, follow step 3; do not thaw wontons before cooking. Follow step 4.

Makes 6–8 servings

FIRE POT
HUO KUO ▪ Mongolia

火　煱

10 cups chicken broth
1 pound sirloin tip, chipped or sliced paper-thin
1 whole chicken breast, skinned, boned, and sliced paper-thin
½ pound medium shrimp, shelled, deveined, washed and butterflied
   (illustration, page 55)
½ pound fresh chicken livers, sliced
½ pound fresh fillet of flounder or sole, sliced
½ pound fresh oysters, washed in salt water and drained well
1 pound fresh spinach leaves, washed and drained well
4 ounces bean threads, soaked in hot water for 5 minutes, drained, and
   cut into 4-inch lengths

DIPPING SAUCE:
¼ cup soy sauce
1 tablespoon sesame-seed oil
1 tablespoon rice wine or dry sherry
½ teaspoon sugar
1 tablespoon minced scallion
1 tablespoon minced parsley

1. Prepare beef, chicken, shrimp, livers, flounder, oysters, spinach, and bean threads and place on separate plate.

2. Mix the dipping sauce.

3. Boil chicken broth in a large saucepan; pour into fire pot. (If using charcoal fire pot, charcoal should be lit at least 10 minutes ahead of time to have white ash formed on briquettes. If using alcohol or sterno, just light it. An electric deep-fryer or frying pan will suffice.) Keep broth at full boil throughout the meal.

4. Arrange plates of ingredients around the fire pot and give each guest a bowl of dipping sauce. Traditionally, the food should be cooked at the table. Guests use chopsticks, fondue forks, or wire strainer to cook tidbits in broth about 20 seconds, then dip in sauce, and eat. When all food has been consumed, the leftover broth can be served as soup.

NOTE: 1. Any raw meat, seafood, or vegetables, cut paper-thin, can be used
     for fire pot.
    2. Fire pot should be kept half full at all times. Add more broth or
    water, as necessary.

TO PREPARE AHEAD: Follow step 1 and refrigerate. To complete, follow steps 2 and 3.

Makes 4–6 servings

RICE, NOODLES, AND EGGS

BOILED RICE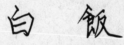
PAI FAN ▪ National

1 cup long-grain rice
2½ cups cold water

1. Combine the rice and 2½ cups water in covered medium-sized saucepan. Bring to boil and immediately reduce heat to medium. Cook 10 minutes or until liquid is absorbed. Reduce heat to low and simmer 20 minutes. Do not stir rice during cooking. Remove from heat.
2. Let rice rest, covered, 10 minutes. Stir with fork or chopsticks to fluff and separate grains.

NOTE: 1. If additional rice is needed, add only one cup water for each cup of rice added.
2. Buy uncooked long-grain rice. Do not wash the rice unless the label tells you to do so. Washing the rice causes the loss of some vitamins and nutrients. If rice has been washed, add only 1 inch of water above level of rice in pot.
3. Converted rice and instant rice are not adequate substitutes. Soggy and lacking texture, they will spoil your dish.

TO PREPARE AHEAD: Follow steps 1 and 2; refrigerate up to one week. Before serving, steam 10 minutes.

Makes 2½ cups

CURRIED-CHICKEN RICE
CHIA LI GEE FAN ▪ Canton

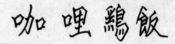

1 whole chicken breast
4 tablespoons peanut or other salad oil
1 tablespoon curry powder
1 cup chopped onion
1 cup chopped celery
1 teaspoon salt
Dash of pepper
2 cups long-grain rice
3½ cups chicken broth

MARINADE:
2 teaspoons cornstarch
½ teaspoon salt
1 tablespoon soy sauce
1 tablespoon rice wine or dry sherry

1. Skin and bone the chicken breast. Cut into ½-inch cubes.
2. Mix marinade and add chicken, tossing to coat. Cover and chill 15 minutes.
3. Heat 3 tablespoons of oil in a wok or skillet until very hot. Stir-fry chicken for 30 seconds. Drain.
4. Heat remaining tablespoon of oil over high heat. Add curry powder, onion, celery, salt, and pepper; stir-fry 1 minute. Return chicken and mix well.
5. Combine rice and chicken broth in a medium saucepan; cover and bring to a boil. Reduce heat to medium; keep cooking 10 minutes or until liquid is absorbed. Pour chicken mixture on top and reduce heat to low. Cover and simmer for 20 minutes.
6. Toss to mix and serve hot.

TO PREPARE AHEAD: Follow steps 1–6; refrigerate. Before serving, reheat 45 minutes in 350-degree oven.

Makes 2–4 servings

GREEN JADE FRIED RICE
FEI TSUI CH'AO FAN ▪ Szechuan

6 tablespoons peanut or other salad oil
4 eggs, well beaten
1 10-ounce box frozen chopped spinach, thawed and squeezed dry
1 teaspoon salt
4 cups packed, cooked rice, cold (page 133)
2 tablespoons soy sauce
2 cooked Chinese sausages (see note), chopped, or ¼ cup cooked, chopped ham
2 scallions, chopped fine, stems included

1. Heat 3 tablespoons of oil in a wok or skillet until very hot. Stir-fry eggs 30 seconds until firm, like scrambled eggs. Remove and chop.

2. Heat remaining oil in a wok or large skillet. Stir-fry spinach 2 minutes. Add salt and rice; stir-fry 2 minutes. Add soy sauce, ham, scallions, and eggs; mix well, and serve hot.

NOTE: To cook Chinese sausages, steam 30 minutes.

TO PREPARE AHEAD: Follow steps 1 and 2; refrigerate. Before serving, cover and reheat 15–20 minutes in a 350-degree oven, or stir-fry until hot.

Makes 4–6 servings

SHRIMP FRIED RICE
HSIA JEN CHAO FAN ▪ National

蝦仁炒飯

1 pound small shrimp, shelled, deveined, washed, and patted dry
9 tablespoons peanut or other salad oil
4 eggs, well beaten
1 cup chopped onion
½ cup chopped bamboo shoots
2 teaspoons salt
4 cups packed, cooked rice, cold (page 133)
2 tablespoons soy sauce
2 scallions, chopped fine, stems included

MARINADE:
2 tablespoons rice wine or dry sherry
½ teaspoon salt
2 tablespoons cornstarch
1 teaspoon sesame-seed oil
2 tablespoons peanut or other salad oil
Dash of white pepper

1. Mix marinade and add shrimp, tossing to coat well. Cover and chill 1 hour minimum or overnight.
2. Mix 2 tablespoons oil into marinade to separate shrimp.
3. Heat 3 tablespoons oil in a wok or skillet until very hot. Stir-fry eggs 30 seconds until firm, like scrambled eggs. Remove and cut into small pieces.
4. Heat 3 tablespoons of oil in a wok or skillet over high heat. Stir-fry shrimp 1 minute until pink. Drain.
5. Heat 1 tablespoon of oil in a wok or skillet. Stir-fry onion until transparent, about 30 seconds. Add bamboo shoots and salt; stir-fry 30 seconds. Add cold rice, stir constantly 2 minutes. Add soy sauce, shrimp, egg, and scallions, mix well and serve hot.

TO PREPARE AHEAD: Follow steps 1–5 and refrigerate. Before serving, reheat in wok or skillet.

Makes 4–6 servings

YANGCHOW FRIED RICE
YANGCHOW CHAO FAN ▪ Shanghai

揚州炒飯

7 tablespoons peanut or other salad oil
4 large eggs, well beaten
1 cup chopped onion
¼ cup diced cooked ham
½ chicken breast
½ pound small shrimp, shelled, deveined, and washed
1 Chinese sausage, cooked (see note), and diced (optional)
4 cups packed cooked rice (see page 133), cold
2 teaspoons salt
3 tablespoons soy sauce
2 scallions, chopped fine, including stems
Dash of pepper

MARINADE:
½ teaspoon sugar
½ teaspoon salt
2 teaspoons cornstarch
1 tablespoon rice wine or dry sherry
1 teaspoon sesame-seed oil

1. Skin, bone, and cut chicken into ⅓-inch cubes.
2. Mix marinade and add chicken and shrimp, tossing to coat. Marinate 15 minutes.
3. Heat ¼ cup of oil in a wok or large skillet until very hot. Stir-fry eggs 30 seconds, until firm, like scrambled eggs.
4. Heat 2 tablespoons oil; stir-fry chicken and shrimp 30 seconds. Drain.
5. Heat remaining oil over high heat and stir-fry onions until transparent. Add ham, chicken, shrimp, and sausage; stir-fry 1 minute. Add rice and salt and stir constantly 2 minutes. Add soy sauce, scallions, pepper, and egg; mix well. Serve hot.

NOTE: To cook Chinese sausage, steam 30 minutes.

TO PREPARE AHEAD: Follow steps 1–6 and refrigerate. Before serving, reheat 15 minutes in a 350-degree oven or stir-fry until hot.

Makes 4–6 servings

COOKED EGG NOODLES
CHU MEIN ▪ National

1 pound fresh egg noddles or ½ pound dried thin egg noodles
1 gallon water
2 teaspoons salt

1. Boil the water in a deep pot. Add salt, then gradually add fresh noodles, stirring constantly. Cook uncovered 1–2 minutes (4 minutes for dried egg noodles) until *al dente*.

2. Drain in a colander and rinse under cold running water to stop cooking and to prevent noodles from sticking together. Drain again.

NOTE: 1. These can be used for any noodle recipe.
2. Noodles should not be overcooked.

TO PREPARE AHEAD: Follow steps 1 and 2; refrigerate 2–3 days or freeze up to one month. Thaw before using.

Makes 6 cups

LONG-LIFE NOODLE
CHANG SHOW MEIN ▪ Shanghai

6 cups cooked noodles (page 138)
1 pound sirloin tip
8 tablespoons peanut or other salad oil
2 cups sliced Chinese cabbage
1 cup sliced celery
½ pound fresh bean sprouts
4 dried Chinese black mushrooms, soaked in hot water 20 minutes,
   stemmed, and sliced
2 scallions, chopped, including stems
1½ teaspoons salt
4 tablespoons soy sauce
2 tablespoons rice wine or dry sherry
¼ cup chicken broth or water
1 tablespoon cornstarch dissolved in 2 tablespoons cold water

MARINADE:
2 tablespoons soy sauce
2 tablespoons rice wine or dry sherry
½ teaspoon salt
½ teaspoon sugar
¼ teaspoon baking soda
1 teaspoon sesame-seed oil
1 tablespoon cornstarch dissolved in 2 tablespoons cold water
Dash of pepper

1. Cook noodles.
2. Slice the beef against the grain ⅛-inch thick and julienne.
3. Mix marinade and add beef, tossing to coat. Cover and chill 1 hour minimum.
4. Add 1 tablespoon of oil to marinade to separate pieces of beef.
5. Heat 3 tablespoons of oil in a wok or skillet until very hot. Stir-fry beef 1 minute. Drain.
6. Heat 2 tablespoons of oil in a wok or skillet. Add cabbage, celery, bean sprouts, mushrooms, and scallions; stir-fry 1 minute. Add salt, 2 tablespoons soy sauce, and rice wine; stir-fry 1 minute. Add ¼ cup chicken broth. Add dissolved cornstarch; stir constantly until sauce thickens. Return beef; mix well. Remove and keep warm.
7. Put remaining 2 tablespoons of oil over high heat. Add noodles and remaining 2 tablespoons soy sauce; stir-fry 2 minutes. Place on heated platter and cover with meat mixture. Serve hot.

TO PREPARE AHEAD: Follow steps 1–4 and refrigerate. Before serving, follow steps 5–7.

Makes 4 servings

SAN SZE NOODLE
SAN SZE LIANG MEIN ▪ Szechuan

三絲涼麵

6 cups cooked noodles (page 138)
1 tablespoon peanut or other salad oil
½ cup julienned cooked lean pork
½ cup julienned cooked chicken
½ cup julienned cooked ham
½ cup shredded bamboo shoots
¼ cup shredded Szechuan pickle

SEASONING SAUCE:
1 tablespoon minced garlic
1 tablespoon minced fresh ginger
⅓ cup cold water
1 tablespoon sesame-seed paste (page 41) or 2 tablespoons peanut butter
1 tablespoon hot-pepper oil (page 62)
1 tablespoon sesame-seed oil
3 tablespoons cider vinegar
⅓ cup soy sauce
2 teaspoons sugar
¼ teaspoon salt

1. Prepare the sesame-seed paste and hot-pepper oil.
2. Prepare noodles and add 1 tablespoon of oil; mix well and allow to cool.
3. Combine garlic, ginger, and cold water in a small bowl; mash with a spoon. Strain, reserving juice and discarding sediment.
4. Place sesame-seed paste in a small mixing bowl. Add garlic and ginger juice, one teaspoon at a time; mix well. Add hot-pepper oil, sesame oil, vinegar, soy sauce, sugar, and salt. Mix well.
5. Pour two-thirds of the sauce over noodles and mix well.
6. Remove to a heated serving platter and cover with meat mixture.
7. Pour remaining sauce on top and serve cold.

TO PREPARE AHEAD: Follow steps 1–4 and refrigerate. Follow steps 5 and 6; refrigerate. On serving, follow step 7.

Makes 6–8 servings

STIR-FRIED RICE STICKS
CH'AO MI FEN ▪ Fukien

炒米粉

⅔ pound small shrimp, shelled, deveined, washed, and patted dry
⅓ pound beef, julienned
1 pound rice sticks
6 tablespoons peanut or other salad oil
4 tablespoons sliced Chinese celery cabbage
½ cup shredded bamboo shoots
⅔ teaspoon salt
1 teaspoon sugar
4 tablespoons soy sauce
1 tablespoon rice wine or dry sherry
⅓ cup chicken broth

MARINADE FOR SHRIMP:
1 teaspoon salt
¼ teaspoon sugar
Dash of white pepper
1 tablespoon cornstarch dissolved in 2 tablespoons rice wine or dry sherry

MARINADE FOR BEEF:
2 teaspoons cornstarch
1 tablespoon rice wine or dry sherry
¼ teaspoon salt

1. Mix shrimp marinade and add shrimp, tossing to coat well. Marinate 20 minutes.
2. Mix beef marinade and add beef, tossing to coat well. Marinate 20 minutes.
3. Soak rice stick noodles 5 minutes in cold water and drain thoroughly.
4. Heat 4 tablespoons of oil in a wok or skillet until very hot. Stir-fry shrimp and beef 1 minute. Drain.
5. Heat remaining 2 tablespoons of oil over high heat. Add cabbage and bamboo shoots; stir-fry 2 minutes. Blend in salt, sugar, soy sauce, rice wine, and chicken broth; bring to a boil and stir constantly 1 minute. Add rice sticks; stir constantly 1 minute. Mix in shrimp and meat. Serve hot.

TO PREPARE AHEAD: Follow steps 1–2 and refrigerate. Before serving, follow steps 3–5.

Makes 4 servings

EMPRESS CRAB MEAT
KUEI FEI SHISH JOU ▪ Peking

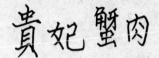

Peanut or other salad oil for deep-frying
¼ pound rice sticks
6 tablespoons peanut or other salad oil
⅓ cup chopped water chestnuts
⅓ cup chopped cooked ham
2 scallions, chopped, including stems
2 teaspoons minced fresh ginger
⅓ pound king crab meat cut into ½-inch cubes

CREAM SAUCE:
½ cup evaporated milk
1 tablespoon cornstarch
8 egg whites, well beaten
1 tablespoon rice wine or dry sherry
1 teaspoon salt
4 tablespoons peanut or other salad oil

1. Heat 3 inches of oil in a wok or deep-fryer to 400 degrees. Add one piece of rice stick to test the oil: Within 3 seconds the rice stick should puff up. Deep-fry rice sticks 5 seconds or so on each side until light brown. Drain and allow to cool. Break into 1-inch pieces and arrange on serving platter.

2. Heat 2 tablespoons of oil in a wok or skillet. Add water chestnuts, ham, scallions, ginger, and crab meat; stir-fry 1 minute. Drain.

3. Mix evaporated milk, cornstarch, egg whites, rice wine, and salt. Add crab meat mixture and mix sauce well.

4. Heat 4 tablespoons of oil in a wok or skillet until very hot. Stir-fry sauce until egg whites begin to set. Pour over rice sticks. Serve immediately.

TO PREPARE AHEAD: Follow steps 1 and 2; refrigerate. Before serving, follow steps 3 and 4.

Makes 2–4 servings

HALF-MOON EGG WITH CRAB MEAT

HO PAO TAN ▪ Peking

荷包蛋

4 tablespoons peanut or other salad oil
8 eggs

FILLING:
2 tablespoons peanut or other salad oil
¼ pound crab meat
1 scallion, chopped, including stems
⅓ cup chopped water chestnuts
1 tablespoon rice wine or dry sherry
½ teaspoon salt
Dash of pepper
2 teaspoons cornstarch dissolved in 2 tablespoons cold water

SEASONING SAUCE:
1 scallion, chopped, including stems
1 clove garlic, minced
1 dried chili pepper, crushed
⅛ teaspoon salt
1½ teaspoons sugar
2 teaspoons cider vinegar
2 teaspoons rice wine or dry sherry
2 tablespoons soy sauce

1. Heat 2 tablespoons of oil in a wok or skillet over high heat. Add crab meat, scallion, water chestnuts, rice wine, salt and pepper; stir-fry 1 minute. Add dissolved cornstarch, stirring constantly until sauce thickens. Remove and set aside.

2. Mix seasoning sauce.

3. Heat 2 tablespoons of oil in wok or small skillet over medium heat. Add 1 egg, sunny-side up. Break the yolk to receive 1 tablespoon crab mixture. When slightly set, fold the egg in half and fry both sides light brown. Drain. Fry remaining eggs one by one, adding oil as needed.

4. Arrange eggs in a skillet over medium heat and pour in seasoning sauce. Cook eggs 3 minutes each side. Serve hot.

TO PREPARE AHEAD: Follow steps 1–3 and refrigerate. Before serving, follow step 4.

Makes 4 servings

SCRAMBLED EGGS WITH SHRIMP
HSIA JEN CH'AO TAN ■ Peking

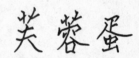

6 eggs, slightly beaten
½ teaspoon salt
2 scallions, chopped, including stems
4 tablespoons peanut or other salad oil
¼ pound small shrimp, shelled, deveined, and washed

   1. Mix the eggs, salt, and scallions.
   2. Heat 4 tablespoons oil in a wok or a skillet until very hot. Stir-fry shrimp 20 seconds. Pour egg mixture over the shrimp and stir-fry (about 1 minute) until the eggs are just set. Serve immediately.

Makes 2–4 servings

SHRIMP EGG FOO YUNG
FOO YUNG TAN ■ Canton

6 tablespoons peanut or other salad oil
1 clove garlic, minced
½ cup chopped onion
½ cup chopped celery
½ pound fresh bean sprouts, rinsed in cold water and drained well
3 dried Chinese black mushrooms, soaked in hot water for 15 minutes, stemmed, and chopped
½ pound small shrimp, shelled, deveined, and washed
1½ teaspoons salt
1 tablespoon soy sauce
Dash of white pepper
4 large eggs, slightly beaten

SAUCE:
¼ cup sliced fresh mushrooms
1 cup chicken or beef broth
½ teaspoon salt
1 teaspoon soy sauce
1 tablespoon cornstarch dissolved in 2 tablespoons cold water

   1. Heat 1 tablespoon of oil in a wok or skillet until very hot. Add garlic, onion, celery, bean sprouts, and chopped Chinese mushrooms; stir-fry 1 minute. Add shrimp, salt, soy sauce, and pepper; stir-fry 1 minute. Drain well and allow to cool.
   2. Pour eggs into the stir-fried mixture and mix well.
   3. Heat 1 tablespoon oil in a wok or skillet over medium-low heat. Pan-fry ½ cup egg mixture on both sides until eggs set and are lightly browned. Drain. Pan-fry remainder, adding oil as needed.
   4. Mix sauce in a small saucepan. Cook, stirring constantly, until sauce thickens and boils. Pour over Egg Foo Yung. Serve hot.

NOTE: Chicken, crab meat, shredded pork, beef, or turkey may be used instead of shrimp.

TO PREPARE AHEAD: Follow steps 1–3, undercooking slightly at step 3. Before serving, cover with foil and reheat 5–8 minutes in a preheated 250-degree oven. Follow step 4.

Makes 2–4 servings

DESERTS 甜 點

ALMOND COOKIES
SHING YAN PEN ■ National

杏仁餅

3 cups all-purpose flour
½ teaspoon baking soda
1 cup margarine or shortening, at room temperature
1 cup sugar
1 egg
2 tablespoons corn syrup or honey
1 tablespoon almond extract
1 egg, well beaten
½ cup blanched whole almonds

1. Sift flour with baking soda.
2. Cream margarine and sugar until the mixture is light.
3. Add egg, corn syrup, and almond extract; mix well.
4. Blend in flour to form dough.
5. Divide dough in half; shape each half into a long roll 1½ inches in diameter. Slice into 1-inch sections and roll each into balls. Space balls 2 inches apart on a greased cookie sheet.
6. Brush tops with beaten egg and lightly press an almond into each ball.
7. Place on top rack in a preheated 350-degree oven; bake 10–15 minutes or until light brown.

TO PREPARE AHEAD: Follow steps 1–7 and freeze.

Makes 2½ dozen

ALMOND WAFERS
SHIH YAN PIEN ▪ National

杏仁片

½ cup butter or margarine, at room temperature
½ cup sugar
1 egg
⅔ cup sifted all-purpose flour
2 teaspoons almond extract
1 cup sliced almonds

1. Cream together butter, sugar, and egg until very light and fluffy.
2. Mix in flour and almond extract.
3. Carefully fold in almonds.
4. Drop by the teaspoonful, 3 inches apart, on a well-greased cookie sheet and flatten drops with the back of a spoon.
5. Place on top rack of a preheated 400-degree oven; bake 4–6 minutes or until light brown around the edges. Remove the cookies with a spatula while still hot; allow to cool on racks.

TO PREPARE AHEAD: Follow steps 1–5 and store in air-tight container.

Makes 2 dozen

EIGHT-TREASURE RICE PUDDING
PA PAO FAN ▪ Shanghai

2 cups sweet rice
2½ cups cold water
4 tablespoons sugar
1 tablespoon shortening

GARNISH:
¼ cup drained maraschino cherries
½ cup drained Mandarin oranges
½ cup drained pineapple chunks
6 dates, halved and pitted
2 tablespoons raisins

SAUCE:
1½ cups cold water
¼ cup sugar
1 teaspoon almond extract
1½ tablespoons cornstarch dissolved in 3 tablespoons cold water

DATE FILLING:
1 pound pitted dates
1 cup water

1. Cook dates in 1 cup water over low heat, covered, until water evaporates and dates are soft. Remove from heat and mash dates. Set aside.

2. Grease an ovenproof 1½-quart mixing bowl (about 8 inches in diameter) with shortening and chill 10 minutes. Spread cherries, oranges, pineapple chunks, date halves, and raisins evenly over bottom.

3. Wash rice in cold water and drain. Combine rice and 2½ cups water in a 3-quart saucepan. Cover and bring to a boil; reduce heat and simmer 15 minutes. When done, stir in 4 tablespoons sugar while rice is still hot.

4. While rice is still hot, divide in half. Carefully spread one half over fruit in the mixing bowl, pushing it up the sides, leaving a well in the center. Press rice down firmly with a wet spoon. Fill well with date mixture and cover carefully with remaining rice. Steam pudding 45 minutes.

5. To unmold, dip a rubber spatula in cold water and gently loosen the edges of pudding. Invert on a serving platter.

6. To make the sauce, boil water and sugar in a small saucepan. Add almond extract and dissolved cornstarch, stirring constantly until sauce thickens and boils. Pour over the unmolded pudding. Serve hot.

TO PREPARE AHEAD: Follow steps 1–4 and refrigerate. Before serving, re-steam 10 minutes. Follow steps 5 and 6.

Makes 4–6 servings

FRIED BANANA
CHA SHIANG CHIAO ▪ National

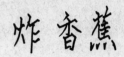

5 bananas
½ cup red bean paste
¼ cup all-purpose flour
Peanut or other salad oil for deep-frying
Granulated sugar for serving

BATTER:
¼ cup flour
¼ cup cornstarch
¼ cup sweet rice flour
½ teaspoon baking powder
1 egg yolk
1 tablespoon peanut or other salad oil
½ cup cold water

1. Peel the bananas and cut in half crosswise; then very carefully butter-fly-cut each half (illustration, page 55).
2. Stuff with red bean paste.
3. Flour stuffed bananas.
4. Combine batter ingredients in a mixing bowl and mix until free of lumps.
5. Heat 3 inches of oil to 350 degrees in a wok or dutch oven. Pierce each banana half with two bamboo skewers. Using skewers as handles, dip bananas into batter and fry until golden brown. Serve immediately with granulated sugar.

TO PREPARE AHEAD: Follow steps 1–5, frying to light brown only, and refrigerate. Before serving, refry until golden brown.

Makes 2–4 servings

FRIED CREAM BALLS
PE TAN SHA WENG ▪ Canton

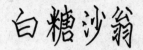

1 cup water
Dash of salt
4 tablespoons butter or margarine
1 lemon or orange rind, grated
2 tablespoons sugar
1 cup sifted all-purpose flour
2 eggs
3 egg yolks
¼ cup chopped walnuts
Oil for deep-frying
⅓ cup granulated sugar
¼ cup toasted crushed sesame seeds (page 41)

1. Bring to a boil the water, salt, butter, lemon rind, and sugar. Add flour all at once; remove from heat and stir with a wooden spoon until mixture forms a ball.

2. Return the pan to very low heat; continue stirring vigorously until the dough becomes dry and leaves the sides and bottom of the pan. Remove from heat and cool 5 minutes.

3. Add eggs and egg yolks alternately, one at a time, beating each vigorously into dough with an electric mixer.

4. When all the eggs and yolks have been added, continue to beat vigorously until dough begins to blister. (This is the secret of the dough's lightness. It takes about 5 minutes with an electric mixer.)

5. Add walnuts and mix well.

6. Heat 2–3 inches oil to 375 degrees in a wok or deep-fryer over medium heat. Drop the dough in by the teaspoonful. Fry a few drops at a time, turning them occasionally until well puffed and golden brown. Remove with slotted spoon and drain.

7. Toss in a bag with sugar and crushed sesame seeds, coating well. Serve warm or at room temperature.

TO PREPARE AHEAD: Follow steps 1–7 and store in paper bag.

Makes 3½ dozen

LYCHEE FLAMBÉ CAKE
HUO SHAO LI SHIH ▪ National

火燒荔枝糕

2 tablespoons shortening
⅔ cup sugar
3 egg yolks
⅓ cup sifted all-purpose flour
1 grated lemon rind
¼ cup lemon juice
1½ cups milk
3 egg whites, stiffly beaten

LYCHEE SAUCE:
1 cup syrup from canned lychees
½ cup water
¼ cup sugar
1½ tablespoons cornstarch dissolved in 3 tablespoons cold water
1 20-ounce can lychees, drained
¼ cup rum

1. Cream shortening. Add sugar and mix well. Add egg yolks one at a time, beating until smooth. Add flour and mix well. Mix in lemon rind and lemon juice. Slowly mix in milk and fold in egg whites.

2. Pour batter into a well-greased 8-inch square cake pan. Set in a large shallow pan with ½-inch depth of hot water. Bake in a preheated 350-degree oven 45 minutes or until golden brown. Turn off heat and let stand in oven 30 minutes. Serve hot or cold with lychee sauce.

3. To make the sauce, combine lychee syrup, water, and sugar in a stainless-steel pan and bring to a boil. Add dissolved cornstarch, stirring constantly until sauce thickens and boils. Add lychees. Remove from heat and mix well.

4. Pour sauce into a heatproof bowl. Heat rum in a small metal pan and carefully ignite hot rum and pour over sauce. Pour over cake. Serve immediately.

NOTE: Lychee sauce can also be served over vanilla ice cream.

TO PREPARE AHEAD: Follow steps 1 and 2 a few days ahead; refrigerate. Immediately before serving, follow steps 3 and 4.

Makes 6–8 servings

PINE-NUT CREAM
SUNG TZU LO ▪ Peking

松子酪

1⅓ cup pine nuts
3 cups cold water
½ cup sugar
¼ cup rice powder
2 cups boiling water
1 tablespoon almond extract

1. Toast or fry the pine nuts in a saucepan over low heat, stirring constantly until light brown. Allow to cool.

2. Put cold water and 1 cup of pine nuts in blender; blend at high speed 1 minute.

3. Combine mixture with sugar, rice powder, and boiling water; cook over medium heat, stirring constantly until sauce thickens and boils. (If a thinner sauce is preferred, increase water.) Serve hot, garnished with remaining toasted pine nuts.

TO PREPARE AHEAD: Follow steps 1–3; reheat before serving.

Makes 6–8 servings

SESAME-SEED COOKIES
CHIH MA BEN ▪ National

2 cups unsifted all-purpose flour
1 teaspoon baking powder
¼ teaspoon salt
½ cup margarine, at room temperature
½ cup sugar
1 egg or 2 egg yolks
1 egg, well beaten
½ cup sesame seeds

   1. Sift flour with baking powder and salt.
   2. Cream margarine and sugar until light and fluffy. Add 1 egg and blend well. Gradually add flour mixture, blending well.
   3. Shape dough into 2 long rolls 1 to 1½ inches in diameter. Wrap and chill 1 hour in freezer.
   4. Slice ⅓-inch thick and space slices ½-inch apart on a greased cookie sheet. Brush with beaten egg and coat with sesame seeds.
   5. Bake on the top rack of a preheated 375-degree oven 15 minutes or until light brown.

TO PREPARE AHEAD: Follow steps 1–3 and freeze. To complete, thaw and follow steps 4 and 5. Cookies may be frozen after baking.

Makes 3 dozen

❉ INDEX ❉